# HORNBY magazine

# What's inside...

'Britain's Biggest Model Railway' - Heaton Lodge Junction - features in this Yearbook as a complete circuit. Read the full story on pages 6-17.

58

# WHO DID IT?

**EDITORIAL**
**Editor:** Mike Wild
**Assistant Editor:** Mark Chivers
**Associate Editor:** Richard Watson
**Sub Editor:** Andy Roden
**Contributors:** Evan Green-Hughes, Tim Shackleton, Trevor Jones and Ian Wild.
**Senior designer:** Steve Diggle

**REGISTERED OFFICE**
Units 1-4, Gwash Way Industrial Estate, Ryhall Road, Stamford, Lincs PE9 1XP

**PUBLISHING**
**Head of Production:** Janet Watkins
**Head of Design:** Steve Donovan
**Head of Advertising Sales:** Brodie Baxter
**Head of E-Commerce:** Martin Steele
**Head of Finance:** Nigel Cronin
**Chief Publishing Officer:** Jonathan Jackson
**Chief Digital Officer:** Vicky Macey
**Chief Content & Commercial Officer:** Mark Elliott
**Group CEO:** Adrian Cox
**Circulation Manager:** Amy Donkersley

**PRINTING**
Melita Press, Malta.

**ADVERTISING**
Advertising: Brodie Baxter
Email: brodie.baxter@keypublishing.com
Tel: 01780 755131  Fax: 01780 757261

 **KEY PUBLISHING LTD,**
Units 1-4, Gwash Way Industrial Estate, Ryhall Road Stamford, Lincs PE9 1XP

# *Welcome*

For this year's Yearbook project layout we have turned our attention to the Great Central Railway's 'London Extension' to build a typical station with an island platform and design cues from a number of locations and trackplans. A Robinson 'O4' 2-8-0 leads a string of empty mineral wagons through the station as a Thompson 'B1' 4-6-0 rolls into the platform with a northbound passenger working.

WELCOME TO THE 2021 *Hornby Magazine Yearbook*. While 2020 has been a challenging year for everyone, we want to put that aside as much as possible to focus on the brilliance of our hobby. There are positives to take from this year, the model railway business has been booming with reports from around the scene that retailers, both mainstream and specialist, have seen an up turn in orders and interest.

Model railways are an ideal means of escapism, a way to enjoy free time and revel in the possiblities of a miniature world. This is what drives the *Hornby Magazine* team, making those miniature worlds come to life on paper and video for modellers of all levels to enjoy and, hopefully, inspire you to take the next step.

The team have been busy behind the scenes creating a brand new model railway for this Yearbook and you can read the full story behind our Great Central Railway (GCR) project inside in two features. It has been another rewarding layout to build, but the limted timescale available to meet print deadlines means that we already have a list of future plans to enrich and improve upon what we have built so far.

Building a GCR layout has long been on our list of ideas and having spent many hours at the preserved Loughborough-Leicester North section we had a good idea of what we wanted to build. Nevertheless, creating a layout with a greater connection to reality took more research than some of our other projects which was another enjoyable part of the process.

Beyond the GCR build we have a wide selection of features covering a range of modelling techniques from weathering to scratchbuilding as well as looking back to the highlights of 2020 and looking forward to 2021 and beyond in our detailed survey of new model projects.

Plus we have been back to see 'Britain's Biggest Model Railway' - Simon George's huge 200ft long model of Heaton Lodge Junction in 'O' gauge - now that he has completed the full circuit for this awe inspiring model railway. You can read about, and, see the full layout on pages 6-17.

The biggest highlight for many in 2020 must be Hornby's Centenary, as the year marked 100 years since Hornby made its first 'O' gauge tinplate locomotives and rolling stock in 1920. It's humbling to think just how far model manufacturing standards have come since then and equally astonishing to think of the detail, variety and operational value which is now installed into every ready-to-run product - it is easy to take that for granted at times.

We are rounding off Hornby's 100th year celebrations with a special feature to cover all the centenary range products as well as highlights of those extra special announcements from the year.

The *Hornby Magazine* 2021 Yearbook is full to the rafters with model railway inspiration, and innovations too, and we hope you enjoy reading and viewing all that we have put together.

We hope all of our readers are staying safe and well and we look forward to meeting with you in the future at model railway exhibitions around the country.

Happy modelling!

**Mike Wild**
**Editor,** *Hornby Magazine*

# Heaton Lodge Junction
# FULL CIRCLE

Britain's Biggest Model Railway first featured in *Hornby Magazine* in Spring 2020 when it was only partly built, but now its builder has completed the circuit. **MIKE WILD** pays a return visit to catch up with **SIMON GEORGE'S** progress on the outstanding Heaton Lodge Junction in 'O' gauge.

**PHOTOGRAPHY, MIKE WILD**

**1** Right: **Class 37** 37191 growls past the sewage works with a block rake of 45ton TTA tankers. This train has been weathered with frost to suggest a chilly start to its journey across the Pennines.

**2** Below: **At Heaton Lodge Junction** split-headcode Class 40 40126 powers up the gradient on the Huddersfield line from the dive-under as a Class 56 leads a loaded MGR train towards the crossover from the Calder Valley route.

WE ALL HAVE A DREAM layout in mind, and I would hazard a guess that most would have an idea of how big it would be, the era it would be set and what it would offer if money, space and time were no object. Few of us would get the chance to create that dream layout, but Simon George is following that path in creating what is described as 'Britain's Biggest Model Railway'.

Housed in the basement of a former mill building in West Yorkshire, just a few miles from the real location, this giant 'O' gauge layout models Heaton Lodge Junction where the Calder Valley and Standedge routes join together with a dive-under which takes one line under the other. The West Yorkshire location has seen several revisions over the years, with Simon's huge 200ft x 50ft layout recreating it as it was in the 1980s when BR blue ruled the day.

The '80s were the time Simon spent his time watching train movements at Heaton Lodge - a time when Class 40s and 45s were still regular traction on passenger and parcel workings, while the screaming V16 turbo engines of the Class 56 were a daily sight at the head of heavy coal trains. His original plan had been to recreate the location in 'OO' gauge which would have required around 90ft to model the 1/3 scale miles in full. However, to model the spectacle of heavy trains hard at work he saw no better choice of scale than 'O' gauge. "The bigger 'O' gauge models had much more momentum compared with 'OO', and even though it meant more space would be needed to build the layout it was an easy choice," Simon commented.

It wasn't an easy beginning for the layout as initially the first boards were built in his double garage at home, but it soon outgrew that typical 16ft x 16ft space that we might savour at home. Simon searched high and low for a suitable premises and by chance had a conversation with a mill owner who showed him a huge redundant basement area. It needed complete renovation from years of disuse, a challenge which Simon took on himself including painting the walls and ceiling white, painting the floor, installing lighting, building a central office and workshop space and cleaning up debris. The effort was well worth it as the mill basement provides the perfect hidden location for his huge model »

📷3 Left: The gas cylinder compound adds a pocket of detail at the junction.

📷4 Right: Both bridges over the River Calder have been modelled with the later steel structure correctly recreated without track as it was in the era. The Class 40 is kit built.

📷5 Below: In a busy scene, a Class 40 heads towards Huddersfield via the dive-under as Class 31 31175 rumbles east towards Leeds. On the high level a Class 56 has charge of an empty MGR on the freight lines heading towards the Standedge route.

railway project which occupies the full length and around half the width of the space available.

The layout models the line from the bridge around ¼ mile east of the junction, the junction itself, the dive-under and the bridges over the River Calder and it all started at the east end. "I started here at the bridge before Mirfield as that is where as a 12-year-old I sat. The whole idea behind this is to replicate exactly the place that I used to go as a kid. I wanted to stand by the railway and take myself back to the '80s when I used to visit the location."

This layout is big like no other. The eye can barely see the detail in the distance at the other end of the scenic section and, in fact, it is 80ft from the bridge at the east of the trackplan to the start of the junction. No other layout we have seen has that sense of distance in quite the same way, though we have been lucky enough to see the spectacles of Over Peover (*Hornby Magazine Yearbook No. 12*) and Roy Jackson's wonderful model of Retford in 'EM' gauge, both of which had a considerable sense of distance.

Everything about Heaton Lodge is big. The scenic section is tremendous, but this is backed by an equally impressive junction, scale gradients, a huge 28-train storage yard, a comprehensive computer control system and much more besides.

## On location

The real Heaton Lodge Junction is in West Yorkshire between Huddersfield and Mirfield. It is the point where the Standedge and Calder Valley lines join together having traversed the Pennines via their two separate routes. The Standedge route offers the most direct means of travelling from Manchester to Leeds via Standedge Tunnel, Marsden, Huddersfield, Heaton Lodge, Mirfield and Dewsbury while the Calder Valley line takes a more circuitous deviation via Todmorden and Brighouse to reach Heaton Lodge Junction to complete the journey to Leeds.

The junction has been through several revisions over the years including being the point that the London & North Western Railway's 'Leeds New Line' diverged to provide an alternative route for trains from Huddersfield to reach Leeds. It added much needed capacity at the time of its opening in 1900, but was later removed as part of the Beeching era cuts in 1965.

Nevertheless, Heaton Lodge continued to be

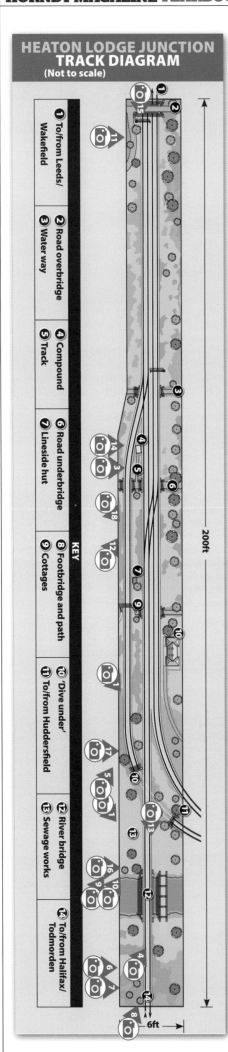

### HEATON LODGE JUNCTION
### TRACK DIAGRAM
(Not to scale)

**KEY**

1 To/from Leeds/ Wakefield
2 Road overbridge
3 Water way
4 Compound
5 Track
6 Road underbridge
7 Lineside hut
8 Footbridge and path
9 Cottages
10 'Dive under'
11 To/from Huddersfield
12 River bridge
13 Sewage works
14 To/from Halifax/ Todmorden

200ft

6ft

📷 6   This Oxford Diecast Mini has clearly seen better days. Simon modelled it as an abandoned and vandalised car outside the redundant sewage works buildings.

an important railway junction with heavy freight traffic vying for paths in between the express and stopping trains. The dive under route from the 'New' line was reinstated in 1970 to take traffic from Huddersfield under the Calder Valley line to reach Heaton Lodge Junction, again increasing capacity, and it stayed in this form until the early 1980s when the Wakefield bound goods line was removed. It is in this form that Simon has modelled Heaton Lodge, prior to the 1980s remodelling, when four tracks approached from the east and split into six at Heaton Lodge North Junction. The northern pair went down a gradient to the dive-under to reach Huddersfield and Manchester while the four tracks continued straight through for a short distance before splitting into two for the Calder Valley Line and two for Huddersfield which joined with those from the dive-under. It's a complex arrangement and one which makes it appealing to model. The dive-under will look particularly impressive when express trains can burst out of the tunnel and climb the gradient to the junction as a heavy coal train passes in the opposite direction destined for the Calder Valley.

The 1990s saw further rationalisation at Heaton Lodge with the dive-under being reduced to a single track at the same time as the chord for west bound trains heading for Huddersfield.

Today Heaton Lodge is set for new changes as part of the electrification scheme on the Trans Pennine route which will see more revisions to its appearance in the coming months and years.

## The details

Impressively though, this isn't just a 'big picture' layout – Simon has really gone to town on the detail elements of Heaton Lodge to create the most authentic replica he can in model form.

The 1980s setting is based in winter with frost getting heavier the further west you go towards the River Calder. The cold winter sun rising in the east is only having a gentle effect on the morning's frost.

Creating the winter look took a lot of practice. Simon spent a year experimenting with static grasses before settling on a final mix to recreate the sense of season. Three different lengths and colours of MiniNatur static grasses are used on the layout. Simon commented: "I've used so much static grass from MiniNatur that they now send it over in bin liners for use on the layout."

Beyond the winter grass there is much to appreciate, and one of the most obvious lineside details is the concrete cable trunking running alongside the running lines. There are two sections of this on the opening four track main line part and that increases ≫

📷 7   A Yorkshire Water Sherpa van has been despatched to take care of a sign replacement to warn off the vandals.

The magnitude of Heaton Lodge Junction is hard to explain – 200ft is a long way on a model railway, even in 'O' gauge. Look closely at this image and in the far distance at the east bridge is a Class 101 DMU heading towards Wakefield while a Class 56 is peeling off towards Huddersfield on the right. The Calder Valley is busy with freight trains as an MGR crosses the Calder destined for Healey Mills yard and a Class 40 begins its assault of the gradients towards Todmorden with a mixed van and open freight.

Class 40 40126 ambles past the sewage works light engine, heading east to Healey Mills Yard.

to three after the junction diverges and Simon estimates that there is at least 600ft of concrete trunking on the layout.

Now consider 600ft and consider making and installing every single piece individually – that's what Simon did. The trunking is made from Evergreen styrene channel section with cable laid into it to represent the real deal along the railway. To give it more character, the lids were left off sections along the way and all were painted concrete colour and set into the superbly laid ballast which surrounds the main lines.

Look closer still and more details come to life. The sharp eyed will spot Tesco plastic bags blown on the trackbed, leaves which have fallen from trees, puddles and streams with debris thrown into them and even vandalised disused signal cabinets. You will even see crops of bracken, but few would realise the lengths which Simon went to create them. "The bracken is etched brass which was shaped, painted and planted individually over three weeks," chimes Simon. "It drove me mad, but I like the effect and I'm glad I did it."

The distinctive gorse bushes are based around a Polak product. Each was covered with additional green coloured flock with the addition of yellow for flowers, as Simon understands that this type of foliage flowers during winter.

The lineside detailing continues throughout the layout including working cranks on the points, Track Circuit Transmitters in true 1980s style, dummy Westinghouse point motors, speed restriction signs, redundant sections of rail, drains, loose bricks and much more besides. The track features outstanding attention to detail including a combination of wood and concrete sleepers while the weathered finish is nothing short of superb and mimics the finest micro layouts on the grandest of scales. This is perhaps one of Heaton Lodge's greatest successes, that on such a monumentally huge model railway Simon has been consistent in his approach to everything by trialling techniques before committing to the final method for use on the layout.

## The new frontier

At the time of our first visit to Britain's Biggest Model Railway in January 2020, Simon had completed around two-thirds of the scenic

The chatter of a Sulzer engine fills the still morning air as it passes Cooper Bridge sewage works and joins the Calder Valley route at Heaton Lodge Junction.

section, but there was still another 30ft of scenery to be completed – that's considerably larger than most exhibition layouts in their entirety.

The latest section models the dive-under tunnel mouths immediately after the 1900 built footbridge which originally crossed the 'Leeds New Line'. This structure still stands today and Simon built the model using a Churchward kit from etched brass. The cottages behind the bridge still stand today and the owner has even been to see the layout in development.

Simon's aim in replicating the dive-under was to make it look decrepit and run down, just as it was in the era. Graffiti on the brick walls, damaged concrete fence panels, mould and damp all surround the tunnels and give it a highly realistic appearance.

Above the tunnel mouths is the Calder Valley line and the four aspect signal which was often used to hold freights for passenger trains to »

**11** The owner of the Capri will need to wait for his windscreen to clear before he sets off. It gets cold at Heaton Lodge in winter.

📷 12 An express crosses on to the Huddersfield line at Heaton Lodge in the hands of a split headcode Class 40. Note the attention to detail in the concrete cable trunking – there is 600ft of it on the layout – spilt ballast, leaves and even frost on the rail sides.

pass underneath and use the junction first. Like all the signals on the layout, this was built by Absolute Aspects and it is fully operational.

Next alongside the line is a snapshot of the huge Cooper Bridge sewage works. It features three sewage treatment beds and ultimately the heads on these will rotate under power. The security fencing is by Buzz Models while close inspection also reveals period Yorkshire Water logos at the site entrance.

The last section is the only fictitious part of the layout. The river bridges are real, but the derelict buildings were built by Allan Downes. Simon adds: "I wanted to include them as a tribute to the late Allan Downes as his work is stunning. The final building before the end of the scenic section is another Allan Downes structure which follows the run-down dilapidated style of the first with smashed glass, debris in the yards and wonderful atmosphere."

Outside the final building is a Mini on bricks which Simon created using a slitting disc in a mini drill to modify the Oxford Diecast donor car. The engine is from a Scania truck which was cut in half to make it fit while the windows are made from microscope slides.

In between the two Allan Downes buildings are the two bridges over the River Calder.

📷 13 Class 56s on coal workings are amongst Simon's favourite memories of the location in the 1980s – their high intensity headlights always gave them away. BR blue livered 56009 crosses the River Calder and slows for the signal check above the dive-under from Huddersfield.

📷 14 Rail workers chat over an oil barrel at the junction compound.

The rear bridge was built in the 1950s, but the rear two tracks were removed soon after in the 1960s and Simon has portrayed the railway as it was in the 1980s with a derelict trackbed over the rear bridge. The front bridge is still in service and carries the double track main line back to the storage yards at the rear.

Scenery is now approaching the final stages which involve detailing the ground cover on the boards in between the junction. These boards are on removable aluminium framed trolleys which allow the boards to be drawn out for maintenance and scenic work. All being well, by the time you read this Simon plans to have the full scenic section complete and all of the remaining 20ft of backscene installed too. He is now also in the final throws of wiring up the track for the dive-under route so that trains can use the full range of route options on Heaton Lodge.

## Trains and operation

Building such a huge model railway creates a big demand for locomotives and rolling stock. Moreover, the gradients of the layout require powerful engines and much of Simon's fleet is drawn from the Heljan range, although there are a number of kit built Class 40 and 56s available too. »

📷15 A centre-headcode Class 40 takes charge of a speedlink working as it approaches the end of the scenic section destined for Healey Mills and beyond.

Highlights include double-headed Class 37s, 40s and 45s on passenger and parcels workings, Class 25s and 31s on goods and secondary passenger work plus the all-important Class 56s for the heavy merry-go-round trains of HAA coal hoppers. In the future more will join the roster including Class 47s and 56s from Heljan as they become available together with more passenger rolling stock to extend the realism of the roster.

Goods stock is heavily influenced by MGR stock with one complete loaded train already in service together with a shorter empty rake. The loaded wagons are Dapol models while the empties are Skytrex kits. There are another 80 MGR wagons in the process of being weathered for the layout which will join the ample rake of Just Like the Real Thing kit built TTA 45ton tankers, Cargowaggon flats, OBA opens and VAA box vans and more, though Simon wishes there was more ready-to-run 1980s period rolling stock available.

At the rear of the layout there is a huge 140ft long storage yard which has four sets of loops,

**16** Left: **Two Allan Downes buildings adorn the latest section to be completed. They are fictitious, but Simon included them as a tribute to Allan's modelling skills.**

**17** Right: **The retaining wall and concrete fencing has been faithfully modelled as it was in the 1980s, complete with damp, mould and graffiti. The banner repeater is soon to become a working item.**

**18** Below: **Passenger workings pace each other at the junction as 31175 climbs up from Huddersfield and 45086 slows to take the crossover to make way for the Brush Type 2. Both are Heljan locomotives.**

one for each main line. Each set has seven tracks which allows the full yard capacity to contain 28 trains for running sessions. It took Simon seven months to build the entire storage yard which features Peco track and DCC Concepts Cobalt point motors.

The layout uses Digital Command Control with a choice of manual or automatic operation. Every train will have a specific siding in the storage yard as its home and will always come back to the same line after passing through the scenic section. The automatic operation will be used when 'Britain's Biggest Model Railway' goes on tour at former department stores across the country and it will control the speed and direction of trains, signals and points through hundreds of sensors which have been positioned underneath the layout.

## The future

Simon's dream of building 'Britain's Biggest Model Railway' is entering its final stages now. The main scenic areas are now complete and, quite impressively, trains can circulate the full layout. It takes up to seven minutes for a scale length MGR to travel all the way around at a scale speed, but what really made Simon want to build a model railway of this magnitude? "The only way to get back the memories of waiting for trains at Heaton Lodge back was to build the layout on a giant scale and for me the layout does that, as it is so long and you have to wait for the trains to come," says Simon.

Big locomotives hauling long trains is the aim of the day and even seeing a handful make their way around Heaton Lodge Junction is an amazing experience. We can't wait to see the full layout out in public on display and its parade of superbly weathered, sound fitted and detailed rolling stock plying through a slice of West Yorkshire countryside as it was in the 1980s. Simply brilliant. ∎

WORKBENCH

# FOUR 'Brits' AND A 'Clan'

The 'Britannia' and 'Clan' 4-6-2s are the subject of this multi-locomotive weathering expedition. **TIM SHACKLETON** presents five BR Standard 'Pacifics' in very different external condition.

THE BR STANDARD 4-6-2s, to my mind, were always a second-class species of 'Pacific'. The Southern's Bulleid 'Pacifics' came into the same category – fine engines but there were so many of them that, for the photographer, they seemed rather common. 'Proper Pacifics' were 'A4s' and 'Duchesses' - high days and holidays locomotives that you saved your last frames of film for. 'Clans' had rarity value – one-off '8P' 71000 *Duke of Gloucester* even more so – but 'Britannias' were perhaps just a little ordinary (better than 'Jubilees' and 'V2s', admittedly, but nothing like as good as an 'A1' or 'A3'). Moreover, they were often pretty scruffy, they were regularly used on freight, they turned up quite frequently at Huddersfield, you got to ride behind them repeatedly and it didn't take long until you'd seen them all.

Nevertheless, I've always been fond of the BR Standard 4-6-2s and the excellent Hornby models of them – and this piece celebrates their diversity. There were myriad minor differences of detail – from smoke deflectors and tender types to coupling rods and livery variations – and some of these will be demonstrated here. My main concern, however, is with their appearance.

The first 'Brit' I can remember seeing was 70049 *Solway Firth* not long after it was named in 1960, and it was filthy. The last was a gleaming 70013

In their final years it was often impossible to tell whether a 'Brit' was in lined green, 'economy green' or what. Unkempt and minus nameplates – the scars came from Railtec Transfers – the former *Lord Rowallan* should by rights have the oval front buffers with which, uniquely among the class, it was fitted in 1966 but it might have helped if I'd checked first that I had some!

*Oliver Cromwell* at Carlisle on the famous '15 Guinea Special' on August 11 1968 that marked the final day of steam operation on British Rail. In between I saw all 55 of them (some of them many times) in all kinds of places and in all kinds of external conditions and that's what we're out to capture here, from shabby, de-named *Lord Rowallan* to a very presentable *Polar Star*.

As ever, I've worked from photographs of the real thing, assiduously copying effects that appealed to me and sometimes migrating them between locomotives. By working on five different models, emphasising some aspects and playing down others, I hope I can show you

how the full spectrum of weathering effects can be applied to these splendid models in a bid to bring them more fully to life. ∎

**WANT TO KNOW MORE?**

● Join us on *www.keymodelworld. com* to watch a sound fitted 'Britannia' in action on our test track and log-in to read the full sound guide from HM161 and more about these locomotives.

# BR Standard 'Pacifics' in retrospect

Left: **Watched by admiring spotters, 70006 *Robert Burns* gets a southbound parcels under way from Doncaster on July 7 1962. From this time onwards, however, 'Britannias' would become increasingly rare on the East Coast Main Line.** Tim Shackleton.

Right: **70047 at Crewe North shed on February 19 1963, its massive BR1D tender perfectly complementing the muscular heft of the locomotive.** Tim Shackleton.

**72009 *Clan Stewart* in the roundhouse at Holbeck after working in over the Settle & Carlisle line on October 5 1963.** Tim Shackleton.

I remember Kingmoor - but on a good day Crewe South could easily produce 20 or more 'Britannias'. 'Clans' were largely confined to Scotland and the North West but there was the odd wanderer – *Clan Stewart* even had a spell working from Stratford shed in 1958.

An immaculate 70013 *Oliver Cromwell* after arrival at Carlisle with the northbound '15 Guinea Special' on August 11 1968. It gave way to two 'Black Fives' for the return journey and then, after servicing, ran light overnight to Diss in Norfolk and preservation at Bressingham Steam Museum.
Tim Shackleton.

## STEP BY STEP **WEATHERING HORNBY 'BRITANNIA' AND 'CLAN' 4-6-2S**

**1** Changing the identity of a locomotive – as I was doing with this project, several times – means removing the factory-applied name and numbers. The easiest way to do this is by gentle rubbing with a fibreglass burnishing brush. I can feel the resale value of this Hornby 'Clan' plummeting and, for the collectors, there's worse to come.

**2** A 'Britannia' livery I've long wanted to model is the unlined green in which a number were outshopped from 1964 onwards. The opportunity came with the acquisition of an all-black locomotive – the form in which, back in 1951, *Britannia* was first presented to officialdom. The big question is: was 'economy green' the same as standard Brunswick green, or a different colour entirely?

**3** It seemed to me at the time that in its unlined form the green looked a very different shade, altogether brighter and less blue. To simulate the effect I wanted it isn't enough to paint the locomotive Brunswick green and omit the lining (I've tried this – it looks wrong). What we need is an impressionist approach, the way an artist would try and recreate a colour no one has seen for 50 years. A process of experimentation led me to settle on a 50:50 mix of Humbrol Dark Green (No 30 – it's actually a mid-green) and Phoenix Precision BR Loco Green (101).

**4** Once the green was dry, I immediately began work on the weathering, with an airbrushed filter coat of 60% Tamiya Red Brown (XF64) with 40% of Flat Black (XF1). This gives a general discoloration over which we can add detail weathering. I usually make several applications, each with a slightly different mix.

**5** Already the locomotive was starting to look right, even without numbers and additional details. This is entirely because of the restraint shown at this critical stage. It's important that you're satisfied before going any further because, if you overdo things, it will be very difficult to reverse out of trouble at a later stage.

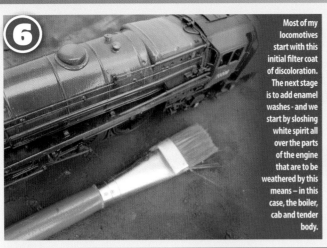

**6** Most of my locomotives start with this initial filter coat of discoloration. The next stage is to add enamel washes - and we start by sloshing white spirit all over the parts of the engine that are to be weathered by this means – in this case, the boiler, cab and tender body.

Intermediate
Beginner **SKILL LEVEL** Advanced

**7** A series of diluted weathering washes (here I used AK Interactive and Revell products in various combinations) can then be painted lightly over the still-wet bodywork. As much as possible is then brushed off, leaving the dirt to accumulate in all the nooks and crannies just as it does in real life. This will create a second layer of weathering over the initial filters. In this case I wanted a middling clean engine so the application was pretty light – the less you put on, the less you need to take off.

**8** It looks pretty crude but paint often does when it's still wet, as it is here. It will soon dry off and settle down. While I was waiting, I hand-brushed a characteristic dribble from one of the washout plugs.

**9** My multiple-layer approach to weathering is a sequential affair, gradually building up the effects I want – or sometimes just letting it happen. Here the first wash has had time to dry and I've added a second one, a paler and more greyish shade. Later on I'll smooth off any rough edges with an airbrush.

*Black Prince* looking pretty good for a 'Brit' in the 1960s. This was very definitely the exception that proved the rule. What a great model this is – all I've done is weather it, mostly using a series of greyish weathering powders from MIG and AK Interactive. Nameplates are from Fox.

**WORKBENCH**

STEP BY STEP **WEATHERING HORNBY 'BRITANNIA' AND 'CLAN' 4-6-2S**

**10** Here, with the 'economy green' locomotive, you can see how a darker, rustier wash has been carefully pooled into the firebox washout plugs – there's water everywhere on a steam locomotive, and where there's water there'll be corrosion. I've sprayed a spot of leakage from the safety valves and gently stroked it downwards by hand brushing.

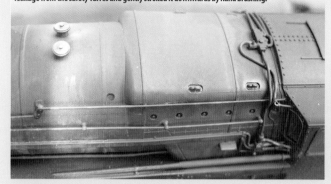

**11** On the tender, the wash has been carefully removed by pulling it downwards with a flat brush. It's collected around the lines of rivets but plenty of the plain green livery remains visible – hopefully it will provoke discussion!

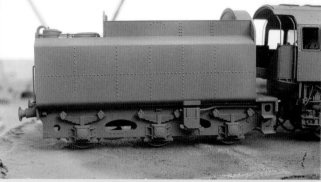

**12** I used the same technique on the lined tender of the 'Clan' – one of the last 'Pacifics' to retain the earlier style of emblem. The bright lining immediately calms down and looks more authentic, especially where it's been obscured by accumulated dirt. The two greens now don't look all that different.

**13** Once I'm satisfied with how the wash process has worked – note the careful build-up of streaking along the boiler – I can airbrush a little more of the acrylic grime filter to mask any rough patches and suggest further dirt build-up. It's incredibly easy to overdo weathering effects, and I can't emphasise enough how important it is to exercise care and restraint.

**14**

Centrifugal force often causes a thin film of oil from the motion to build up on the wheels. If you have an airbrush, this is very simple to replicate – just spray on a thin coat of satin varnish. Let it dry and then repeat if necessary.

**15** Wanting to reproduce an end-of-life locomotive on which not a hint of green remained visible, I used just sufficient paint to obscure the underlying livery and lining – and no more. As ever, self-control is vital – to represent leakage from the safety valves I've used just the faintest misting with an airbrush, followed by fine brushwork. There are actually three colours here, all different shades of grey-beige. Used on its own, pure white looks far too stark.

70009, the former *Alfred the Great*, in the controversial 'economy green' livery of the mid-1960s. It may have been the same shade of green BR always used but, without the orange lining, it certainly didn't look the same. The location is Carlisle Kingmoor, the date 30 April 1966. *Keith Chester.*

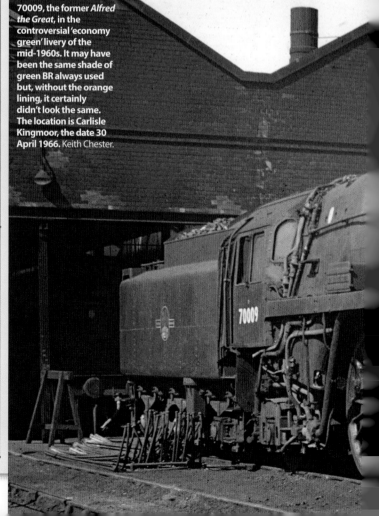

Intermediate

Beginner **SKILL LEVEL** Advanced

 **16** Don't forget to airbrush a sooty black along the top of the boiler – like all weathering, this will help pick out the details of the fittings.

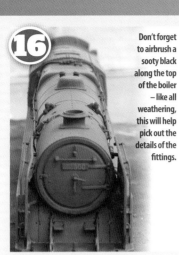

**17** Now we're starting to get somewhere. Still to be treated with weathering powders, but clearly showing the effect of filters and washes, 72009 *Clan Stewart* glints in the evening sunlight. The 'Clans' operated in soft-water areas and showed little evidence of the limescaling that was such a problem further south.

**18** By way of contrast, *Polar Star* is immaculate, with the factory finish enhanced by a thin coat of gloss varnish and just a hint of clean dirt in all the right places, such as below the running plate and around the firebox and related pipework. Again, an exercise in restraint as much as anything. If you've only ever seen preserved steam locomotives, you'd be forgiven for thinking they always looked like this. They didn't.

**19**

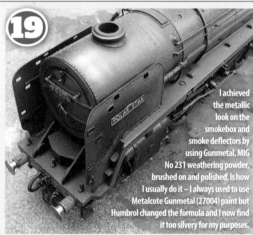

I achieved the metallic look on the smokebox and smoke deflectors by using Gunmetal. MIG No 231 weathering powder, brushed on and polished, is how I usually do it – I always used to use Metalcote Gunmetal (27004) paint but Humbrol changed the formula and I now find it too silvery for my purposes.

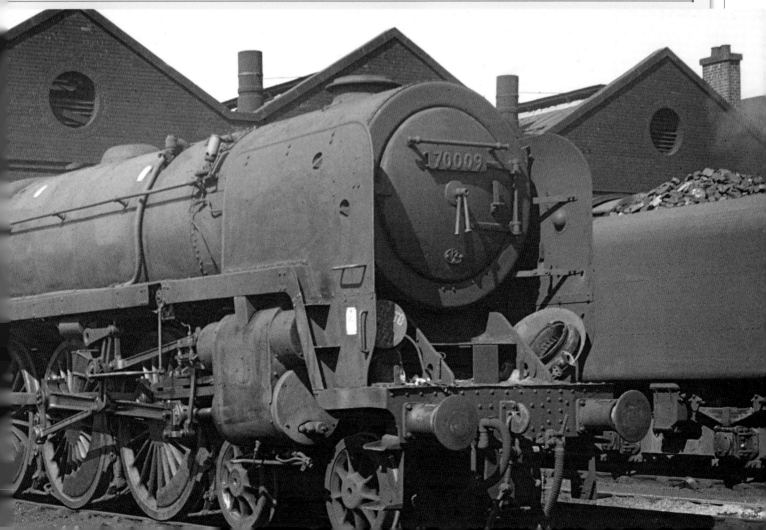

# THE BR STANDARDS

In recent years, no group of locomotives has been so intensively modelled as the British Railways Standard classes, developed by the newly-nationalised railway in the early years of its existence. **EVAN GREEN-HUGHES** finds out why they were designed and looks at the engineering challenges that resulted.

# 1948 WAS A MOMENTOUS year for the nation.

Many of the promises of the new post-war Labour Government were beginning to come to fruition and there was a general feeling that at last things would begin to get better for the average man in the street. One of the major planks of Labour party policy had been the nationalisation of the railways, something that was very popular with the public, but less so within the business community.

As midnight struck on January 1 that year, railwaymen all over the country sounded the whistles of their engines in celebration but that act merely reflected the problems besetting the industry. All of the whistles made different noises and even on this relatively minor issue there was absolutely no nationwide agreement.

The Government had dictated that an Executive should be formed which would take control of the railways and, as part of this process, a team of engineers was put together whose brief included the instruction to introduce common standards across the network. On the locomotive front, Robert Riddles was appointed member of the Executive with responsibility for rolling stock and his principal assistants were to be R.C. Bond and E.S. Cox. All three had worked together before and all three came from the London Midland & Scottish Railway, a move that would have a profound influence on the development of the Standard steam engines but which was unlikely to find favour with senior engineers from the other three railways.

## The 1948 exchanges

A locomotive standards committee was then set up, which was chaired by a A.W.J. Diamond, a former Great Western man, and this was given the task of producing suggestions for the types of locomotive that would be required. Work also commenced to find out what were the relative merits of the designs which were already in service. Trials were organised in which five express passenger engines, four mixed traffic and four heavy freight locomotives from BR's constituent companies were pitted against each other, in many cases by examples being sent onto 'foreign' lines. This move saw such remarkable sights as a GWR 'King' and a Southern 'Merchant Navy' working on the East Coast Main Line and an 'A4' class 4-6-2 and a rebuilt 'Royal Scot' working expresses from Waterloo on the Southern. While the results were very interesting, it is safe to say that no one design of locomotive was conclusively better than any other in the same power class, and while some had better features than others there was not one that shone above all the rest. »

In a fantastic display of power, BR '9F' 2-10-0 92180 leaves Hadley Wood North Tunnel with a down goods on August 4 1962. These highly successful heavy freight locomotives weren't originally part of the BR Standard plan, but they proved their value in service on both freight and passenger work.
Ken Cook/Rail Archive Stephenson.

However, this work did have a useful outcome in that the Locomotive Standards Committee was able to start work on designing a range of standard fittings which would include such items as boiler mountings, valves and controls. From this it was able to supply the committee with data which was then used to draw up a range of potential standard specifications which could be used to build a range of locomotives capable of covering all duties on the railways. Obviously, development of new locomotives would take some time and so it was agreed that while this took place, a number of locomotives would be constructed to existing designs from the previous 'Big Four' - in part to keep Works building and also to fulfil orders placed before nationalisation. Many of these were mixed traffic types such as the LMS 'Black Five', the GWR 'Hall' and the LNER's 'B1' – all mixed traffic 4-6-0s - but there were some express engines built, too, particularly by the Eastern Region. The only type of locomotive that was not constructed was for heavy freight, because there was a ready supply of ex-War Department 2-8-0s of LMS and WD design available. Of interest in the light of later developments was that some locomotives of LMS design were built specifically for use on other regions as part of this programme.

## Setting standards

The committee proposed that British Railways should consider building six types of standard engine, with the initial proposals containing neither express passenger nor heavy freight designs, as there was thought to be enough existing so as not to warrant further construction. Two types of large mixed traffic tender engines were included, the biggest of which would be a 'Pacific' 4-6-2 or a 4-6-0 with the smaller being a 4-6-0 or a 2-6-0. There were to be two mixed traffic tank engines which would be either 2-6-2Ts or 2-6-4Ts, with a light freight 2-6-0 or 0-6-0 for pure goods work also proposed. The final design was for a small 0-4-0 suitable for work on tightly-curved dock complexes.

Along with these proposals, a policy was developed which would see future locomotives built with as many parts interchangeable as possible, and with others designed so that tooling intended for one class could be used to construct another. This was not a new idea and many railways had been moving in this direction for several decades.

A decision was also taken to adopt relatively conservative design principles, particularly those of the LMS and the GWR, which meant an end to some of the innovations promoted by designers

such as Bulleid of the Southern and an end to the construction of complex multi-cylinder locomotives as favoured by the LNER. Given the success and modernity of some LMS designs compared with equivalents from the other three railways, it was always likely that many of the proposed engines would be Crewe-inspired.

By this time there had been a rethink of what was required and Cox came up with a revised list of 12 potential designs which would form the basis of all future steam locomotive construction. Of these, four would be completely new, four would be developments of existing types and four would be existing designs that would receive only detailed modification. The four new designs were put forward because it was felt that sufficient advances could be made over what already existed, and at this stage they comprised of two 'Pacifics', which would be more or less identical, except that one would have 6ft 6in driving wheels and be intended for express passenger work while the other would have 6ft 0in drivers and would be for mixed traffic. The third design would be a mixed traffic 4-6-0 with the fourth being a freight 2-8-2. The latter would have shared the same design of boiler, which would have been smaller than the 'Pacifics' and which would have given them a wide route availability.

Developed from existing designs were to have been a Class 8 4-6-2, a 4-6-0 and 2-6-0 for mixed traffic and a 2-6-2T, while modified existing designs, which were exclusively LMS in origin, were two types of 2-6-0 tender engine, a 2-6-2T and a 2-6-4T.

It soon became apparent that two 'Pacific' designs, differing only in wheel size, could not be justified and therefore the pragmatic decision

Above: **The 'Britannia' class 'Pacifics' were the first of the new BR Standard to enter traffic. Their ergonomic cabs were a revelation to crews which made them easy and comfortable to operate. 70051 *Firth of Forth* is turned on Patricroft turntable in April 1963.**
Jim Carter/Railphotoprints.uk.

Below: **BR '4MT' 2-6-4T 80122 departs Stirling with the 3.39pm train to Edinburgh Princes Street in September 1960. The '4MT' 2-6-4Ts were purposeful and capable locomotives which could accelerate rapidly on suburban services.**
W.J. Verden Anderson/Rail Archive Stephenson.

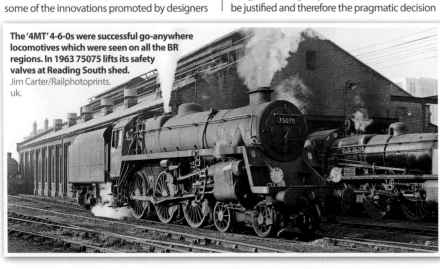

**The '4MT' 4-6-0s were successful go-anywhere locomotives which were seen on all the BR regions. In 1963 75075 lifts its safety valves at Reading South shed.**
Jim Carter/Railphotoprints.uk.

was taken to build only one class, but with driving wheels at the compromise size of 6ft 2in, which would still enable high-speed running to be undertaken. At the same time, the new 4-6-0 was to be upgraded to be more powerful and would be placed on a 4-6-2 frame, but because of its smaller boiler and wheels would provide a locomotive with a much lower axle load. The same cylinders, wheels and valve gear would then be used to make a more powerful 4-6-0, but this would have the boiler from the LMS 'Black Five' instead of the proposed Standard design. On the freight front, the proposal for a 2-8-2 did not find much favour, especially as Riddles had had a great deal of success with his 2-8-0 and 2-10-0 locomotives for the War Department, and in light of this the design evolved into a 2-10-0 which would have a wide firebox and 5ft diameter driving wheels.

### First builds

As far as the modified designs were concerned three went ahead straight away, these being the '4MT' 4-6-0, the '3MT' 2-6-0 and a 2-6-2T, with all being very heavily influenced by LMS practice. The proposal for a large express engine was shelved as there was not a requirement at that time and it was not dusted off until some years later when 71000 *Duke of Gloucester* was built in 1954. The final four designs were straight LMS copies, being BR versions of the Ivatt '2MT' and

| BR STANDARD STEAM LOCOMOTIVES | | | |
|---|---|---|---|
| **CLASS** | **NUMBERS** | **WHEEL ARRANGEMENT** | **NUMBER BUILT** |
| 'Britannia' | 70000-70054 | 4-6-2 | 55 |
| '8P' | 71000 | 4-6-2 | 1 |
| 'Clan' | 72000-72009 | 4-6-2 | 10 |
| '5MT' | 73000-73171 | 4-6-0 | 172 |
| '4MT' | 75000-75079 | 4-6-0 | 80 |
| '4MT' | 76000-76114 | 2-6-0 | 115 |
| '3MT' | 77000-77019 | 2-6-0 | 20 |
| '2MT' | 78000-78064 | 2-6-0 | 65 |
| '4MT' | 80000-80154 | 2-6-4T | 155 |
| '3MT' | 82000-82044 | 2-6-2T | 45 |
| '2MT' | 84000-84029 | 2-6-2T | 30 |
| '9F' | 92000-92250 | 2-10-0 | 251 |
| **Total:** | | | 999 |

'4MT' 2-6-0s, the same designer's '2MT' 2-6-2T and again the well-designed Fairburn 2-6-4T. The first three were built more or less as they had been but the larger tank required considerable modifications to enable it to fit within a more restrictive loading gauge - changes that resulted in the characteristic inclined cylinders which are a prominent feature of these engines.

With the groundwork now comprehensively covered, authorisation was given to commence building ten of the types, with only the larger express passenger 'Pacific' and the freight 2-10-0 put on hold.

Despite the previously-held belief that there were enough express passenger engines priority

was actually given to the construction of the two 'Pacific' classes, followed by the '4MT' 4-6-0. Designers from the works at Brighton, Derby, Doncaster and Swindon were involved in making the drawings for the project. From the outset, a great deal of consideration was given to the use of standard parts with instructions given that this should include wheels (where only six sizes could be used), cylinders (five sizes) and boiler flanging blocks (seven sizes). In addition, the work already done on standardised fittings was to be included with all locomotives expected to have the same cab fittings and general layout.

The original intention was that the Standard locomotives would have main frames made up »

Unfortunately the 'Clan' 4-6-2s weren't as successful as the other Standard steam designs. They were all allocated to the Scottish Region and saw service as far south as Carlisle on a regular basis. 'Clan' 72008 *Clan Macleod* departs from Edinburgh Princes Street station with a stopping train for Glasgow Central in August 1957.
D.T. Greenwood/Rail Archive Stephenson.

BR '3MT' 2-6-2T 82017 arrives at Clapham Junction with the 'Bournemouth Belle' empty coaching stock on July 16 1964.
Brian Stephenson.

of forged or cast steel bars, as used extensively in the USA, rather than the usual steel plate, which was prone to cracking. However, this plan had to be abandoned fairly early on when it was realised that BR's own workshops did not have the equipment or capacity to produce such items, which would in any case have been much heavier than those of a more conventional pattern. Eventually it was decided to use narrow conventional frames but with substantial cross-bracing, with two distinct patterns of frames, one to suit existing boiler designs and one to suit the new BR-built types.

As far as cylinders were concerned, Cox had long been a supporter of the idea of building locomotives with only two outside cylinders. There were many reasons for this, but the most important one was that two-cylinder engines could be more easily maintained as all the motion was outside the frames and was easy to access. The new Standards were to have cylinders which would be as large as could be fitted outside, yet conforming to the existing loading gauge, but this led to difficulty with some of the more powerful engines, meaning the cylinders had to be fitted at an inclined angle in order to get them within the set parameters. Walschaerts valve gear was used all round while the slide bars used were based on the Gresley three-bar design for the larger engines and, where space was at a premium, the single-slide bar arrangement as used by the LMS.

It had originally been proposed that all the new designs would feature boilers fitted with wide fireboxes, but it was soon decided that those engines which were developments, or copies, of existing designs should continue to be fitted with the narrow firebox type already in existence. Four new wide firebox types were designed,

which were for the new 'Pacifics' and the heavy freight 2-10-0, but initially only those for what became the 'Britannia' and the 'Clan' were put into production, the others coming later. Wide fireboxes were preferred because they were more efficient when loaded with indifferent coal and gave a bigger margin of error when badly fired.

Of the existing designs, '5MT' 4-6-0s were given the same boiler as the LMS 'Black Five' while the '4MT' 2-6-0s had that fitted to Ivatt's LMS 'Moguls'. The boiler previously fitted to the Ivatt 2-6-2T found use on the BR Standard '2MT' 2-6-0s and 2-6-2Ts, while the '4MTs' in tender and tank form were given a design similar to that used on the LMS '4MT' 2-6-4Ts. The only major departure from the use of all-LMS hardware was with the '3MT' 2-6-0s and 2-6-2Ts, which used an adapted Swindon No. 2 boiler used on the GWR '51XX' 2-6-2Ts.

## Ergonomic design
A particularly novel feature of the new tender engines was the arrangement by which the cab was attached to the boiler rather than to the locomotive's main frames to reduce vibration on the footplate. This arrangement allowed the cab to be extended backwards so that there was a continuous floor right the way to the tender, eliminating the fallplate, and giving a firm floor for the fireman to work on. The cab itself was a completely new design and had the controls laid out in a more logical fashion than many previous designs. It also included a seated driving position and many other novel features for a steam locomotive cab.

BR's Design Committee also put a lot of thought into the tenders which they would run with their new engines. Only three different types were originally envisaged and all had inset sides which »

There was a significant LMS influence on the BR Standard steam locomotives and most specifically on the '2MT' 2-6-0 and 2-6-2Ts which drew on previous Ivatt designs for their specification and design. '2MT' 2-6-2T 84007 heads away from Seaton under the Midland Main Line with a train for Stamford on April 30 1960. Gordon Hepburn/Rail Archive Stephenson.

allowed engine crew a view down the side of the tender, a small window being put at the back of the cab for the purpose and also to help when running tender first.

Combined with the new cab design, the tender design prevented coal dust from being blown into the cab, at least in less quantities than before. This innovation followed the use of similar tenders by the LMS and must have come as a great relief to some areas, particularly the former GWR, where low-sided tenders with no protection were still in widespread use. Later, this popular feature had to be abandoned as further developments required more coal and water capacity which led to straight sides being used with a top flare, similar to those in use on locomotives such as the 'Duchess' and 'Black Five'.

### Rule 'Britannias'

As with the design, construction of the actual locomotives was shared out between several main Works, with Brighton, Crewe, Darlington, Derby, Doncaster, Horwich and Swindon all being involved. All of these Works had previously built LMS-style 2-8-0s for the War Department and had experience of the general layout and construction of LMS engines. As planned the first locomotive to appear was 'Britannia' 4-6-2 70000 *Britannia* which emerged from Crewe in January 1951. This engine caused a sensation at the time due to its high running plates and sleek appearance, and after a bit of bedding in, it and its later companions began to be well-respected by the enginemen that had to work them.

Construction of Standard locomotives then continued for a period of nine years with 999 being built, ending with the celebrated '9F' 2-10-0 92220 *Evening Star* in 1960. In general terms, all the classes (perhaps bar the 'Clan' 4-6-2s and 71000 in BR service) were a success, although some required modifications, mostly of a minor nature before realising their full potential.

There are many who say that British Railways should not have proceeded with the Standard designs as the writing was on the wall for steam. However, the decision had to be taken in the context of the economic situation at that time, which required reduction as far as possible of imports and the export of as much as possible. Had the decision gone ahead to re-equip with diesels, expensive oil would have had to be brought into the country rather than our locomotives burning home-mined coal.

Riddles and his team also had to grapple with the relative costs of each type of traction because a diesel was up to four times more expensive to build than a steam engine. Perhaps

BR '2MT' 2-6-0 78019, closely based on the Ivatt '2MT', pilots '4MT' 2-6-0 76052 on a Stainmore line goods at Coal Road signalbox in the late 1950s.

more importantly was the requirement to do something about the state of the country's motive power quite quickly and therefore the easiest and most logical solution was to continue with tried and tested technology which could be produced within existing workshops and without comprehensive re-tooling.

Riddles was never a promoter of diesels, except for those which were used for shunting, but instead preferred a traction plan which envisaged steam being used until the money was available to electrify much of the network, with trains then being powered by electricity provided by power stations burning home-mined coal instead of by imported oil. However, his views held sway for only a short time for within three years of the production of the first of his 'standard' steam engines the Railway Executive was abolished and the new order, faced with an increasing operating deficit, saw the only way forward as modernisation. This led to the infamous plan of 1955 being announced, but by this time Riddles had decided to retire.

The Standard steam engines continued in service until the last was withdrawn in 1968. Many of them had scandalously short lives, in many cases lasting less than 10 years - and most were far from worn out when they were taken out of service. However, they were what their designers had intended, which was simple to operate, easy to maintain, economical, robust and had modernisation not interfered would also have been long-lasting too. They were also capable of operating on any region and in many ways set new standards for steam locomotives in Britain which have never been beaten since and probably never will be. ∎

The small fleet of '3MT' 2-6-0s spent their career in Scotland and the North East initially with some finishing their careers on the Southern. 77009 stands on shed at Polmadie Glasgow (66A) in the company of 'Clan' 72002 on July 27 1955.
David Anderson/Railphotoprints.uk.

The BR '5MT' 4-6-0s took ideas from the LMS 'Black Five'. On July 3 1958 '5MT' 73107 steams out of Moncrief Tunnel and approaches Hilton Junction south of Perth with an up express. W.J. Verden Anderson/Rail Archive Stephenson

# KEEP THOSE WAGONS ROLLING!

Having recently completed construction of Railway Laser Lines' 4mm scale Wagon Repair Depot kit, **MARK CHIVERS** was keen to display the finished structure while also keeping options open for its future use, so he developed this 'OO' gauge photographic diorama.

Above: **A solitary BR bauxite HEA hopper stands in the yard in front of the depot building.**

Below: **A Coal sector Class 58 stables in the siding adjacent to the wagon works which is inspecting a pair of Beilhack snowploughs ahead of the winter season.**

A DIORAMA is a great way of showcasing a model in a detailed scene without taking up too much space. With a little planning, you can also keep elements of the diorama temporary enabling the showcase model to be utilised on another scene or layout in the future. Plus, if you haven't got the space to build a complete layout, or you want to test out your modelling skills, a diorama is a great means of exploring your own potential.

With the recently completed 4mm scale laser-cut kit of a wagon repair depot under my belt (HM161), I found myself at the point where I wanted to display the building properly, but a layout scenario was still some way off. So, with a spare offcut of 6mm MDF sheet to hand, a 640mm x 330mm base was cut to size to house the planned scene. The plan was kept simple with just three parallel tracks required as all turnouts would be 'off-scene'.

As I wished to keep the depot building removable, a pencil outline of the structure was drawn on the base for reference. This helps ensure scenic materials and glue are kept away from the structure where possible so it can be easily removed and replaced without affecting the rest of the diorama scene. With the pencil handy, the security fence line and an area of scrubland were also marked on the base.

The completed kit already features a section of 'OO' gauge Peco code 75 flexible track extending from the depot entrance, so three additional lengths were roughly placed on the diorama board until I was happy with their positioning. These were then cut to size, ensuring each length was flush with the end of the diorama board so the scene could potentially be connected to another section in the future. The track was then secured in place with PVA glue, making sure the first length of track was aligned with the depot's main entrance. With hindsight, I should probably have used a strip of 1/16in cork sheet (or similar packing) to lift this section of track, as there was a slight 'lip' between the tops of the rails once the glue was dry.

A security perimeter was next to be installed, using Shedring Hobbies' 4mm scale 3D printed palisade fencing and gates. A large pair of double gates represents the main entrance at one side of the depot, while a smaller pedestrian access gate was installed at the other. To give the depot that in-use appearance, I opted to model the main gates partially open.

Ballast was applied to all but the proposed area of scrubland and secured in place in the usual way with a watered-down PVA solution in a 50:50 mix of water and PVA glue with a drop of detergent added to help it flow into the loose ballast. A mix of Woodland Scenics blended grey fine and medium ballast was used to achieve the look I was after and subsequently toned down with an airbrush loaded with Geoscenics weathering solutions. This step reduces the stark »

MAKING A SCENE

| WHAT WE USED | | |
|---|---|---|
| PRODUCT | SUPPLIER | CAT NO. |
| 4mm scale 3D printed palisade fencing and gates | www.shedringhobbies.co.uk | SR176PSFL001 |
| 4mm scale 3D printed oil barrels | www.shedringhobbies.co.uk | SR176OB001 |
| 4mm scale 3D printed traffic cones | www.shedringhobbies.co.uk | SR176TC001 |
| 4mm scale modern trackside walkway/grating | www.scalemodelscenery.co.uk | LX210-OO |
| 4mm scale wagon repair depot (laser-cut kit) | www.railwaylaserlines.co.uk | RLL101WR |
| Gaugemaster flowering grass tufts | www.gaugemaster.com | GM138 |
| Geoscenics track-oil grime (twin-pack) | www.geoscenics.co.uk | TS50/TG50 |
| Goods and loco depot signage (WR) | www.sankeyscenics.com | BRGLD/W4 |
| Hornby Skaledale portable office ('OO') | www.hornby.com | R8765 |
| Lifecolor rail frame dirt | www.airbrushes.com | UA719 |
| Lifecolor brake dust | www.airbrushes.com | UA724 |
| Green Scenes static grass fibres (various) | www.green-scenes.co.uk | Various |
| Faller 'HO' scale waste bins | www.gaugemaster.com | 180914 |
| Peco code 75 flexible track | www.peco-uk.com | SL-100F |
| Peco rail-built buffer stops | www.peco-uk.com | SL-40 |
| Wild area with bushes – spring | www.model-scene.com | F571 |
| Woodland Scenics grey blend fine ballast | www.bachmann.co.uk | WB1393 |
| Woodland Scenics grey blend medium ballast | www.bachmann.co.uk | WB1394 |

appearance of the freshly laid ballast and gives it a more realistic workstained appearance.

To provide a safe walking route for staff, Scale Model Scenery's 4mm scale modern trackside walkway grates were installed. These were painted before cutting from the fret and glued directly to the ballast with PVA. Extra care was taken at this stage to level any uneven ballast and ensure the grates were aligned correctly. Next, static grass was added to the fence line, beneath buffer stops and the building perimeter, while the area of scrubland was

developed using Model-Scene's impressive range of foliage and bush matting. These are offered in a selection of finishes covering different seasons and appearances. Supplied as a 280mm x 180mm sheet, the material is ready to glue in place but can also be cut to the shape required. I opted for suitably sized strips, teasing the material as necessary before securing with PVA.

For the final finishing flourishes, further detailing was added to bring the diorama to life with oil barrels, traffic cones, waste bins and

general detritus, while a Hornby 'OO' Skaledale portable office building (R8765) was placed close to the depot entrance as a security office and mess room, completing what turned out to be a fun and satisfying project.

The following step by step guide shows how we built this 'OO' gauge Wagon Repair Depot diorama. ∎

Above: **Building a diorama like this is a great way to test your skills and create a means of displaying rolling stock.**

Right: **A Class 08 shunter ticks over outside the Railway Laser Lines Wagon Repair Depot. The laser cut kit has been embedded into a diorama to display it.**

STEP BY STEP **BUILDING A WAGON REPAIR DEPOT DIORAMA**

Intermediate
Beginner **SKILL LEVEL** Advanced

**①**

To create the diorama base, we used 6mm MDF sheet. Having placed the completed Wagon Repair Depot building in position on the MDF sheet, we then measured a 640mm x 330mm panel and cut it to size. Materials were gathered, track was loosely placed in position and the fence line was drawn on the base in pencil

**②**

We used Shedring Hobbies' 4mm scale 3D printed palisade fencing and gates to represent the depot's security perimeter. Whilst they are supplied in grey plastic material, a coating of grey primer was added to tone down their appearance. Allow to dry before adding to the layout.

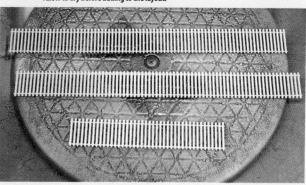

**③**

With the track plan finalised, the fencing was glued in place. A pair of large entrance gates and a pedestrian entrance were also added. Holes were drilled into the board to locate the slightly longer pegs on the gates. All parts were then glued in place with contact adhesive and allowed to dry.

**④**

Next, a coat of PVA glue was added to the depot area ahead of gluing the track in place directly to the baseboard. The first section of track was lined-up with the entrance to the depot and secured. Check the height of the rails match, too - a strip of 1/16in cork sheet may have helped prevent a 'lip' between them in this case.

An Oxford Diecast Ford Transit collects an oil drum and generators from the yard.

**STEPS 5-20**

STEP BY STEP **BUILDING A WAGON REPAIR DEPOT DIORAMA**

**5** As we plan to utilise the depot building on other projects too, we kept glue away from the base of the building so it remains removable. The other lengths of track were cut to size and glued to the baseboard.

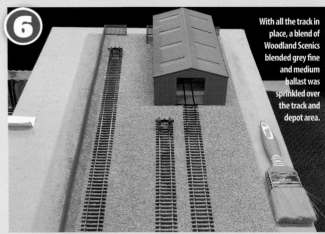

**6** With all the track in place, a blend of Woodland Scenics blended grey fine and medium ballast was sprinkled over the track and depot area.

**7** With the depot area covered, the track ballast was carefully brushed into position with a soft flat brush, removing as much material as possible from the sleeper surfaces.

**8** The areas to the rear of the depot and around the entrance gates were also treated to ballast, ahead of finally fixing it in place with a watered-down mix of PVA glue.

**9** Having first removed the building, mist the ballast with a light coating of water using a spray bottle to aid the next step. Then, with a small syringe, or similar, carefully apply a watered-down mix of PVA in the usual way, ensuring the entire area is treated. Allow to dry overnight.

**10** To tone down the ballasted depot area, a coat of Geoscenics track grime weathering was added with an airbrush. Attention was given to the rail sides, sleepers and walkway areas.

**11** Scale Model Scenery trackside walkway/grating sections were used for the pedestrian route from the main gate to the depot entrance. These were sprayed with Lifecolor brake dust (UA-724) and allowed to dry before each section was cut from the sprue with a sharp craft knife.

**12** Once the application of weathering was dry, the rails were cleaned-up with a track rubber. Model-Scene's range of foliage matting was utilised to create a rough area of land on the other side of the security perimeter. This can be cut from the mat with scissors and teased into position. Fix in place with PVA glue. An area of foliage was added on the depot side too, just to liven up the otherwise flat appearance.

Intermediate

Beginner **SKILL LEVEL** Advanced

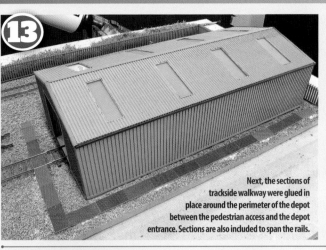

**13** Next, the sections of trackside walkway were glued in place around the perimeter of the depot between the pedestrian access and the depot entrance. Sections are also included to span the rails.

**14** Beads of PVA glue were then added along the depot-side of the fence line, beneath the buffer stops and around the base of the depot building, before a covering of static grass was applied to bed things in.

**15** The scene is really coming together now. A few vehicles from the Oxford Diecast 1:76 range were added for effect, along with the first of the detailing items such as 4mm scale 3D printed oil barrels and Kernow Model Rail Centre's exclusive '00' Bachmann Scenecraft compressor loads.

**16** A Hornby Skaledale '00' portable office building was added to the scene as a security/staff mess room. The original transfers were carefully scraped away and replaced with modern security examples.

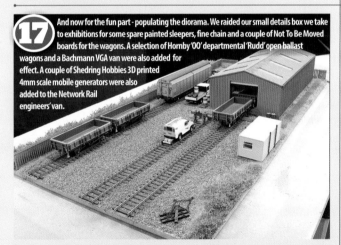

**17** And now for the fun part - populating the diorama. We raided our small details box we take to exhibitions for some spare painted sleepers, fine chain and a couple of Not To Be Moved boards for the wagons. A selection of Hornby '00' departmental 'Rudd' open ballast wagons and a Bachmann VGA van were also added for effect. A couple of Shedring Hobbies 3D printed 4mm scale mobile generators were also added to the Network Rail engineers' van.

**18** Extra details were added to the main entrance. 3D printed traffic cones were placed across the main gate entrance, while a modern waste container from Faller's range of 'HO' scale accessories was also placed close to the entrance. Flowering grass tufts from the Gaugemaster range add extra colour to the scene, while a couple of traffic cones appear to have found a new home.

**19** Further flowering grass tufts and detailing help to complete the scene including further lubricant barrels and pallets.

**20** The completed diorama with engineers' wagons awaiting repair. Note the Not To Be Moved boards on the wagons which were built up from the Sankey Scenics range of 4mm scale signage. The next task will be to add lighting and interior detailing to the Wagon Repair Depot building.

# The Great Central Railway
# THEN AND NOW

The Great Central Railway is a unique survivor in preservation with its signature double-track main line, and this late 1890s built line forms the subject of our feature build for the Yearbook. To begin the 'OO' gauge project, **MIKE WILD** looks back at the 'London Extensions' story with archive images.

'Foreign' motive power was a common occurrence on the GCR with summer Saturday and special workings. In 1964 GWR 'Hall' 4-6-0 6911 *Holker Hall* arrives at Loughborough Central, the terminus of today's Great Central Railway, with a Poole-Bradford summer Saturday express.
Gordon Hepburn/Rail Archive Stephenson.

BR '9F' 2-10-0 92069 thunders through Ruddington (seen from 50 steps bridge) with an Annesley to Woodford Halse 'Windcutter' mineral train on September 20 1963. This location is the current limit of the Great Central Railway Nottingham which will be joined to the southern section in the future.
Gordon Hepburn/Rail Archive Stephenson.

THE THRILL OF STEAM-HAULED trains passing in motion is a rare phenomenon in railway preservation – and even rarer on the main line railway network. But there is one line where steam hauled services pass each other every running day – the Great Central Railway between Loughborough and Leicester North.

Stretching 8 ¼ miles through the Leicestershire countryside, this jewel in the preservation crown is an outstanding testament to the days of steam. Fully signalled stations, original architecture, characterful and extensive goods trains for special events, superb motive power and one of the great spectacles of preservation – mail exchange on the move from a Travelling Post Office van.

The Loughborough-Leicester section is one of two surviving sections of the 1899-completed 'London Extension' of the Great Central Railway main line which ran north from Quainton Road, Buckinghamshire to Nottingham. The second preservation site runs from Ruddington on the outskirts of Nottingham to a link line to the national network via the Midland Main Line at Loughborough. The two railways are working to become one by reinstating the missing link – restoration of the bridge over the Grand Union Canal to the north of the GCR Loughborough station and reconstruction of the bridge over the Midland Main Line to the south of Loughborough's Midland Main Line station. The result will be an 18-mile stretch of the Victorian era GCR reborn for future generations to enjoy which will see trains running from the outskirts of Nottingham to the northern limits of Leicester.

## Birth of the GCR

The GCR main line from Nottingham to London grew out of Sir Edward Watkin's desire to expand the Manchester, Sheffield and Lincolnshire Railway (MS&LR). His vision consisted of a new main line running south to London which could even connect to a channel tunnel for onwards connections to mainland Europe (concerns about opening a possible invasion route stopped this at the time).

It took a few more years for Watkins' original »

Southern Region 'West Country' 4-6-2 34002 *Salisbury* passes Ashby Magna on the Great Central main line with an almost empty M1 Motorway behind. It was in charge of an RCTS special on August 13 1966. Note the family resemblance of the buildings at Ashby Magna compared to those at the present day preserved GCR. Brian Stephenson.

vision to be completed – 96 to be precise, with opening of the Channel Tunnel in 1994 – but he was able to instigate the construction of the 'London Extension' which began the establishment of the Great Central Railway. The new line joined the MS&LR at Annesley, Nottingham, and continued south through Loughborough, Leicester and Rugby before joining with the Metropolitan Railway to complete the route to London through Buckinghamshire at Quainton Road. A diversion was added to take GCR trains into London Marylebone as their southern terminus. The 'London Extension' was completed in 1899 and was the last full main line to be built in Britain until construction of High Speed 1 in 2003 to serve the Channel Tunnel.

In 1905 the joint GCR/Metropolitan route was replaced by a Great Western/Great Central joint line via High Wycombe which offered easier gradients than the original Metropolitan joint route.

In the north the GCR expanded its network to include lines into North Wales accessed via the Cheshire Lines Committee route. The GCR also expanded in North Lincolnshire by establishing the port at Immingham. Work started in 1906 and it opened to great fanfare in 1912 and continues to serve deep sea shipping to this day.

The GCR was an innovative company and highlights included introduction of low pressure hydraulic signalling and completion of the first power operated gravity yard at Wath. This could handle 5,000 wagons per day in two sets of sidings and featured air-operated points.

The GCR's locomotive department was busy too, developing successful designs led by J G Robinson. He joined the GCR in 1900 and became Chief Mechanical Engineer in 1902. His legacy includes the long-standard '8K' (later 'O4' under the LNER) 2-8-0 heavy freight locomotive, the 'Improved Director' 4-4-0s, 'A5' 4-6-2Ts, 'J11' 0-6-0s, 'B5' 4-6-0s and many others. The passenger livery was an ornate lined green scheme while freight locomotives carried a lined black colour scheme. All bar one of Robinson's GCR locomotive designs

joined LNER stock at the 1923 grouping when the company became part of the newly formed London North Eastern Railway.

## Classic features

The GCR's track formation was mainly double track, but one of the 'London Extension's defining features was its island platform station design. This style is typified by Loughborough, Quorn and Rothley stations on the preserved section. The island platforms had access from a road bridge, although Lutterworth was accessed via an underpass to an island platform, and a collection of buildings along the platform including waiting rooms, toilets and booking offices.

Large goods yards were provided with ample space to handle arrivals and departures for interchange between road and rail while in

some cases there were additional goods loops to accommodate holding heavy freights to allow passenger trains to pass. Part of this design provided space for future development which meant there was always space around a GCR station, even in BR days. Often there were wide expanses of cinder ash between the running lines while photographs of the line, even on plain line sections between stations, always show it to be immaculately maintained.

## Fight for survival

Despite all its successful engineering developments, and growth of traffic to and from the port of Immingham (the GCR even had its own fleet of ships), the GCR struggled for traffic on the 'London Extension' from the start but fought hard to gain what it needed to

'Austerity' 2-8-0 90137 passes West Ruislip with a Neasden-Woodford Halse Freight on September 29 1956. It is using the former GCR/ Metropolitan Railway route to reach the Midlands junction.
Dave Cobbe Collection/ Railphotoprints.uk.

The Robinson 'O4' 2-8-0s, originally GCR '8K', were synonymous with the 'London Extension' on freight work and just one of the class of 145 locomotives survives today at the preserved GCR. In 1951 'O4/8' 2-8-0 63827 passes Rugby Central with an up freight from Annesley.
W.J. Verden Anderson/Rail Archive Stephenson.

survive. Its main rival was the Midland Railway (later LMS) operated Midland Main Line from London St Pancras which also passed through strategic locations in the Midlands including Leicester, Loughborough, Nottingham, Sheffield and Manchester. The GCR meanwhile missed population centres with its route and instead passed through more rural locations with attractively named stations including Finmere, Brackley, Woodford Halse, Lutterworth, Ashby Magna, Belgrave and Birstall, Rothley, Quorn and Woodhouse and Ruddington along its route. It also operated Leicester Central, Loughborough Central and Nottingham Victoria stations at its principal towns and cities.

Despite its challenges, the GCR attracted strong traffic for the movement of coal to London as »

well as iron ore for the steel industry, finished steel products and fast fish services from the port of Grimsby to Banbury and Whitland amongst other destinations. Freight traffic kept the line busy, but it also saw stopping and fast services – the latter including the 'South Yorkshireman' train – speeding through countryside to take passengers along the 'London Extension' to reach destinations including Sheffield and Manchester – the latter via the electrified Woodhead Route.

The 1923 grouping brought new motive power to the GCR line including the Gresley 'V2' 2-6-2s and later Thompson's new 'B1' 4-6-0s became regular performers on the line. The ex-GCR Robinson locomotive fleet continued in service under the LNER, but some were rebuilt with a number of 'O4s' being overhauled with a 'B1' boiler and cylinders – amongst other modifications – to become the 'O1' class.

Nationalisation saw the Great Central move into the hands of the British Railways Eastern Region, but it was only to last for 10 years before it was handed over to the Midland Region in 1958. The new management brought different locomotives to the line including Stanier '8F' 2-8-0s together with 'Black Five' and 'Royal Scot' 4-6-0s and BR 'Britannais', and it was also well known for its association with 'WD' 2-8-0s and BR '9F' 2-10-0s. There were also DMUs in the very last years of its existence, though diesel-electrics were rare. Nevertheless, there were unusual visitors including English Electric gas turbine prototype GT3 and also through workings with Bulleid 'Pacifics' from the Southern and Collett 'Hall' 4-6-0s from the Western on inter-regional trains. Another highlight was the Bradford-Poole train which brought Southern Region green stock to

the line turn-about with Midland/Eastern Region stock during the early 1960s bringing a different colour of passenger stock to the line. Railtours and football specials also brought unusual motive power to the line including more of the Southern's 'Pacifics' to the Leicester area.

During the 1960s it was operated by the management of its rival Midland Main Line. With two essentially duplicate routes, in the climate of the times, one would have to go, and the Great Central Main Line was slated for closure in Dr Beeching's report. Intermediate stations were closed from 1963 and freight traffic moved away

to other routes during the decade – a process some would suggest was of deliberately and possibly cynically managed decline. The final section remained between Nottingham and Rugby and soldiered on until the entire 'London Extension' was closed in 1969. Gone now were the stations of Loughborough, Quorn and Woodhouse, Rothley, Belgrave and Birstall, Ashby Magna, Rugby Central, East Leake, Leicester Central and more leaving Sir Edward Watkin's dream in tatters.

Happily, that wasn't the end for the GCR as the Main Line Steam Trust stepped in to re-

The London terminus of the Great Central was Marylebone. Stanier 'Black Five' 44847 stands at Marylebone after arrival with the 8.15am service from Nottingham Victoria in 1965. Hugh Ballantyne/Railphotoprints.uk.

Woodford Halse was a busy junction on the Great Central route with connections to the Great Western network. Stanier '8F' 48027 makes a smoky southbound exit with a lengthy mixed freight on April 18 1964. Neville Simms/Ranwell Collection/Railphotoprints.uk.

establish the section between Loughborough and Leicester North (the latter at the site of demolished Belgrave and Birstall station) which included the original station buildings at Loughborough, Quorn and Woodhouse, and Rothley.

Elsewhere parts of the GCR still remain in daily use today including sections in North Lincolnshire to Immingham while Chiltern Railways operates on the former GWR/GCR joint line through High Wycombe and the former Metropolitan joint line still sees passenger services on some sections and freight only

BR '5MT' 4-6-0 73010 passes over the Midland Main Line at Loughborough as it heads away from Loughborough Central with a holiday express from Portsmouth to Nottingham Victoria on August 10 1963. This bridge, along with its associated embankment is to be reinstated by preservationists as part of the Great Central Railway's reunification plans. Gordon Hepburn/Rail Archive Stephenson.

beyond Aylesbury Vale and through Quainton Road towards Calvert.

## Into preservation

Enthusiasts wanted to keep the former Great Central 'London Extension' open for future generations and following securing of a lease on the Loughborough Central station site in 1970 began the process of preservation. There were significant challenges in its early years, particularly funding to purchase the track from BR, but from 1973 it was able to run trains between Loughborough and Rothley on single track. The Great Central Railway Ltd was formed in 1976, the section from Loughborough to Rothley was saved while Charnwood Borough Council purchased the land to secure the line's future. During the 1980s the GCR extended south to its current terminus just beyond the original station at Belgrave and Birstall on the outskirts of Leicester due to extensive vandalism of the

original station buildings which meant they had to be demolished. The southern terminus is called Leicester North.

Initially the line was single track between each of the stations as volunteers gradually rebuilt the old route. Fortunately, they had the original stations at Loughborough, Quorn and Woodhouse, and Rothley to work with which gave the line instant character. An engineering base was established at Loughborough for locomotives while a carriage and wagon restoration centre is now based at Rothley to keep the railway's fleet in full working order.

Following completion of the line to Leicester North, the GCR's next move was to propose returning the line to double track formation under the leadership of its president David Clarke. The first section to be doubled was between Quorn and Rothley station while this was later extended to include the section north from Quorn to Loughborough. It opened to passenger services on June 1 2000 and since then the railway has continued to flourish.

Loughborough and Quorn are both fully signalled, the latter being completed in 2004, while Quorn also boasts a Travelling Post Office mail exchange point which is demonstrated with high speed steam haulage under strict conditions at events. The line has also been passed for 60mph running for private testing which the railway has been used for by main line locomotive builders in the past.

Another major achievement was the full signalling of Swithland Sidings, situated close to Rothley station. This area has been signalled with GWR style lower quadrants to mimic those seen on the GWR/GCR joint line via High Wycombe. The signalbox at Swithland sidings was relocated from Aylesbury South. It was built by the GWR in 1905, and the scheme was completed in May 2012 and saw the railway receive the National Railway Heritage Awards Signalling Award the same year.

Today the Loughborough-Leicester North section boasts four fully operational signalboxes, three complete 'London Extension' stations »

Woodford Halse allocated 'J11' 0-6-0 64327 waits to leave Nottingham Victoria with a stopping train for Leicester Central on September 12 1954. John P. Wilson/Rail Archive Stephenson.

**Great Central Railway 'London Extension' stations – Nottingham-London Marylebone**

North to Sheffield and Manchester — Nottingham Victoria — Ruddington — Rushcliffe Halt — East Leake — Loughborough Central — Quorn and Woodhouse — Rothley — Belgrave and Birstall — Leicester Central — Narborough Whetstone — Ashby Magna — Lutterworth — Rugby Central — Braunston and Willoughby — Charwelton — Woodford Halse — Culworth — Helmdon — Brackley

and respected locomotive, carriage and wagon and signalling teams to maintain the line. It has also had strong links with the National Railway Museum with the line being home to three National Collection engines – Robinson 'O4' 2-8-0 63601, BR 'Britannia' 4-6-2 70013 *Oliver Cromwell* and SR 'King Arthur' 4-6-0 30777 *Sir Lamiel*. Also in the fleet of locomotives, both operational and awaiting overhaul are examples of the Stanier '8F' 2-8-0 and 'Black Five' 4-6-0, Ivatt and Riddles '2MT' 2-6-0s, Fowler 'Jinty' 0-6-0T, Bulleid 'West Country' 4-6-2, Hawksworth 'Modified Hall' 4-6-0, BR '9F' 2-10-0 and BR '5MT' 4-6-0 on the steam side. There are also resident examples of classes 08, 20, 31, 33, 37, 45 and 47 on the line, while visiting engines are regular too.

## The northern section

However, the 8 ¼ miles from Loughborough to Leicester North is only part of the story, as there is a second preservation operation on the 'London Extension' based at Ruddington on the outskirts of Nottingham. This centre has a large base at Ruddington which connects to the Great Central Main Line trackbed at Ruddington South Junction, just south of the original station site, for a 10-mile journey back along the route through Rushcliffe Halt and the former station at East Leake before reaching the end of its current running line just north of the Midland Main Line in Loughborough.

The most exciting development is that the two railways are now working towards unification by overhauling the Grand Union Canal bridge to the north of Loughborough shed together with

BR '9F' 2-10-0 92093 enters Leicester Central with an Annesley to Woodford 'Windcutter' mineral working on April 7 1964. Gordon Hepburn/Rail Archive Stephenson.

reinstallation of the bridge over the Midland Main Line allowing GCR trains to run between Leicester and Nottingham once more. The full plan also calls for a new locomotive shed for the railway as well as reconstruction of the embankment between the canal bridge and the Midland Main Line. It is a huge project which the Great Central Railway is seeking donations for to allow its dream to become a reality. The latest work has seen the overhaul of the canal bridge completed, including restoration of the original

Beyond Quainton Road the GCR shared the route of the Metropolitan Railway to London, though this route was later supplemented by a joint GWR/GCR line via High Wycombe. On June 3 1939 'A1' 4474 *Victor Wild* passes Wendover with an up express for Marylebone. George C. Lander/Railphotoprints.uk.

| USEFUL LINKS | |
|---|---|
| **Great Central Railway** | *www.gcrailway.co.uk* |
| **Great Central Railway Nottingham** | *www.gcrn.co.uk* |
| **Railway Archive (original trackplans from 1901)** | *www.railwayarchive.org.uk* |
| **Reunification project** | *www.gcrailway.co.uk/unify/* |

Finmere · Calvert · Quainton Road · Akeman Street · Waddesdon Manor · Wotton · Aylesbury · Haddenham · Stoke Mandeville · Princes Risborough · Wendover · West Wycombe · Great Missenden · High Wycombe · Amersham · Beaconsfield · Chalfont and Latimer · Seer Green Halt · Chorleywood · Gerrards Cross · Rickmansworth · Denham · Sandy Lodge · Ruislip · Northwood · Northolt Junction · Pinner · South Harrow · North Harrow · Sudbury and Harrow Road · Wembley Hill · Neasden · London Marylebone

structure and lattice sides.

The next section to be tackled is the 'Factory Flyover' - a combination of brick arches and a metal bridge – to take the railway over a factory entrance which will cost £3 million to complete. This will be followed by reconstruction of the embankment in between, construction of the bridge over the national network, overhauling of the A60 road bridge and work to repair the embankment north of the Midland Main Line. The progress so far is impressive and once complete it will create a tremendous heritage line connecting the outskirts of two major cities with steam haulage. Full details of the GCR reunification project can be found at its dedicated website (see panel).

## The GCR in miniature

Having set the scene, we now need to roll up our sleeves to start building our all-new model of the Great Central theme station. With such a significant and well known legacy we have a lot to live up to, but we have a plan which you can read about next in this Yearbook. ■

**Rebuilt 'Royal Scot' 46163 departs from Nottingham Victoria with the 11.15am van train to Marylebone on August 3 1964. This once grand station no longer stands.** Gordon Hepburn/Rail Archive Stephenson.

**BR 'Britannia' 70012** *John of Gaunt* **departs East Leake with the 5.15pm Nottingham Victoria to Marylebone semi-fast on July 31 1963. East Leake station site still exists today as part of the Great Central Railway Nottingham, though it is completely unrestored.** Gordon Hepburn/Rail Archive Stephenson.

# Building the
# GREAT
**PART ONE**
# CENTRAL RAILWAY

The GCR is well served with locomotives, rolling stock and buildings offering the perfect ingredients to inspire *Hornby Magazine's* Yearbook project. **MIKE WILD** introduces this 'OO' gauge layout and explains its design and first phase of construction using Hattons new range of laser cut baseboards.

**PHOTOGRAPHY, MIKE WILD**

Robinson 'O4' 2-8-0 63598 ambles through Quorn Magna with a long mixed goods while a 'J11' 0-6-0 simmers in the goods yard. Bachmann's Scenecraft buildings recreate the island platform design of the GCR well.

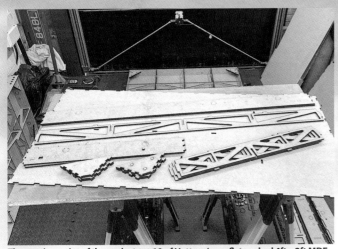

The starting point of the project are 10 of Hattons' new flat packed 4ft x 2ft MDF baseboard kits. This is how each baseboard starts.

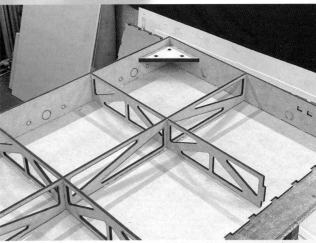

Assembly begins with the inner framework followed by the outer panels. Triangular corner braces add strength and provide a mounting point for legs.

ROBINSON 'O4s' on rakes of mineral wagons, island platforms and wide open spaces are the first things which spring to mind for me when it comes to the Great Central Railway's 'London Extension' between Nottingham and Quainton Road in Buckinghamshire. It was one of the unfortunate main lines in Britain in that it came under the Beeching axe for closure which resulted in the removal of through passenger trains in 1966.

However, as one of the last great main line railways to be built in Britain, apart from the Channel Tunnel Rail Link from London to Folkestone, the GCR holds a special place in history and that is further emphasised by the superb preservation operation between Loughborough Central and Leicester North which survives today. With such a strong legacy via the preserved section of the GCR, we felt it was high time we recreated one of its stations for a new layout.

As we outlined in our introduction to the GCR in this Yearbook, the 'London Extension' had a common design of stations which featured island platforms, matching structures and either a road over bridge or under bridge for access. There were a couple of exceptions to that rule including Rushcliffe Halt but, nevertheless, the line had a feeling of corporate design.

Happily, Bachmann has recognised the value of the GCR, its motive power and its buildings over recent years. It started with the Robinson 'O4' 2-8-0 which it released in 2010 (HM37) offering ➤➤

the first Great Central designed ready-to-run locomotive. It has since been followed by the 'D11' 4-4-0 and 'J11' 0-6-0 from Bachmann together with the Thompson 'O1' 2-8-0 from Hornby, which was an equally prolific freight engine on the GCR main line. There are many other choices for ready-to-run BR era GCR motive power too including Hornby's '8F' 2-8-0, 'Black Five' and 'Royal Scot' 4-6-0s, 'L1' 2-6-4T and 'Britannia' 4-6-2 while Bachmann can add the '9F' 2-10-0, 'WD' 2-8-0, BR '5MT' 4-6-0, 'V2' 2-6-2 and many more. You can read more about the model GCR motive power roster for this layout in a separate feature on pages 96-105. Add to this an attractive range of ready-made structures in the Bachmann Scenecraft range, modelled on Rothley, and we had the raw ingredients to get started

on a project which would rekindle some of the romance and magic of the GCR 'London Extension'.

## The design

Creating the design for the layout started with the concept of a station on one side and a storage yard on the other, a classic exhibition style layout. However, we soon felt that the plan would be restrictive in its operation by constraining the scenic area to just one through station from the GCR, so we decided on a full four sided design which would model a station on one side and replicate Swithland Sidings on the other.

Many of our design cues are taken from the preserved section of the GCR to give the model familiarity, but while it takes inspiration from what remains today, we've also spent many hours researching the

On completion of assembly with PVA wood glue we taped the joints with masking tape to ensure everything stayed in place during drying. The process was then repeated for the remaining nine boards for the layout.

prototype to develop a realistic trackplan for the steam era. This was helped by the online resource

at the Railway Archive which gave access to a full set of GCR trackplans for the line through

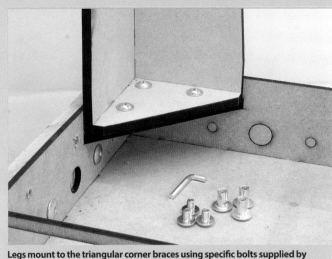
Legs mount to the triangular corner braces using specific bolts supplied by Hattons in the kits. They have allen key heads for easy assembly.

The completed baseboards for the layout bolted together and showing the dropped board for the reservoir scene. We modified one of the 4ft x 2ft boards by adding 12mm MDF panels to one side and end to lower its height.

the county of Leicestershire.

The overall footprint is 16ft x 8ft. Our station, named Quorn Magna – a combination of Quorn and Woodhouse and Ashby Magna, takes much of its inspiration from Quorn on the preserved GCR. Highlights include an island platform with Bachmann's Scenecraft buildings adorning the same manufacturer's platforms, a lie-by siding stretching back from the platform on the outer circuit, a goods yard with two long sidings and inclusion of a goods loop and headshunt.

At the country end of the station side, the line curves around - one of our compromises of making a model railway - with the double track main line running between the lie-by siding and headshunt until it reaches a road overbridge. This is another product from the Bachmann Scenecraft range which models Weybourne bridge on the North Norfolk Railway – it is closely related to bridge styles on the GCR.

After the bridge, the line continues its curve around to the other side by crossing a lower level board which will ultimately model Swithland Reservoir, though with the railway on a curve rather than straight. Next, the line will pass our version of Swithland Sidings which will have the same four-track effect with goods loops either side of the main line together with a handful of sidings behind and a route out for the Mountsorrel branch before completing the circuit back to Quorn Magna.

The first phase of the build featuring here focuses on Quorn Magna station and we will be moving onto Swithland Sidings through *Hornby Magazine*.

## Building the base

Previously our layout projects have used baseboards made from 9mm plywood for the tops and 18mm x 69mm timber for the framework. The method and design has proved reliable and robust over many layouts and exhibitions, but for this layout we wanted to follow a different path to showcase a brand new product range from Hattons.

The baseboards are all assembled from Hattons new 4ft x 2ft MDF laser cut baseboard kits. The parts are neatly cut and supplied flat packed, and have useful features including openings in the internal framework to allow wiring to pass through, baseboard bolts which also align the boards and specifically designed legs which »

Thompson 'O1' 2-8-0 63670 eases a mixed goods around the curve between the lie-by siding and headshunt on the approach to the station. Layered static grasses give great depth to the scenery.

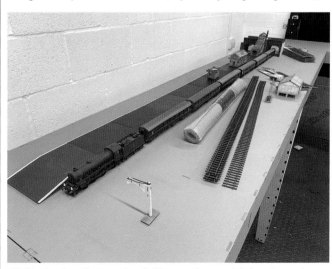
All of the baseboards were painted with grey paint to seal their surface and prepare for track laying using Peco's bullhead track system.

A new railway deck was cut to shape from 6mm MDF and mounted on temporary blocks of 12mm MDF to complete the circuit. This will later be clad to look like Swithland Reservoir viaduct.

A comparison in sleeper spacing between traditional Peco flat bottom rail code 75 track on the left and bullhead code 75 track with scale sleeper spacing on the right. The latter is a vast improvement.

can be fitted with adjustable feet – perfect for sloping garage floors.

The GCR layout used ten of these boards to create the 16ft x 8ft footprint - three for each side and two for each end. We arranged them in this way (rather than four for each side in line and one between the two sides) to make way for the Swithland Reservoir scene. The baseboard kit design means there is no need to use tools during construction (although you will need a hammer to tap pins into the tops of the legs) meaning that all you need to build the boards is a work area and PVA wood glue. Having built ten, we got construction down to a fine art where it was taking around ten minutes to assemble each board.

With a glue assembled board the most important step is allowing it to dry. During this process we added masking tape over the principal mating surfaces to ensure everything stayed where it should. This worked well and meant that after 24 hours we had a solid baseboard ready to be assembled to its legs.

Hattons system for legs is based around the first board in a layout having four legs and all others having just two at one end or side. In practice, this works very well and provides a sturdy layout which is quick to assemble and simple to build.

To make the system of solid top boards work for our plan we needed to be able to incorporate a lower level board for Swithland Reservoir and having throught about the simplest way to achieve that we decided on adding 12mm MDF panels to one side and end of one board which were 180mm deep – 90mm deeper than the board they joined to. These added 12mm to the width and length of the layout which we compensated for by adding a 90mm deep strip of 12mm MDF between the pair of boards at the opposite end and a matching section to one of the station side boards to keep everything square.

The final step in our process before moving onto the track was to paint all of the baseboard surfaces and faces with grey

paint. This acts as a seal for the wood and gives a clean working environment to begin the railway construction process.

## Track changes

For the track on this layout we opted for something new – Peco's code 75 bullhead rail track. While this isn't brand-new to the market right now, it is the first layout that we have built with this type of track. Its advantages are twofold – scale sleeper spacing for more accurate appearance of 'OO' gauge track and the new 'Unifrog' point system which has been generated by the manufacturer. The only downside currently is that there are only large radius left and right-hand points available currently to go with the plain yard lengths of track, but all is not lost for the future as further points are in development to give crossings, slips and medium radius turnouts.

Putting the limitations of point availability aside, we have been totally impressed by the bullhead track system. The scale sleeper spacing makes a big difference

to the appearance of the railway instantly – even before ballasting – while Peco has also gone to the lengths of making tiny rail joiners which even have the bolt head pattern that you would see on the real railway. All-new plastic rail built buffer stops are also available in the product range to complement the track and these are a big step up from the previous design produced for the Streamline track system.

However, the single biggest benefit – particularly for DCC layout builders – are the new 'Unifrog' points. These are entirely live and fully wired to work straight from the box on DCC without the need to employ any insulated rail joiners, even at crossovers. The only reasons you would need to add insulated joiners are if you want to physically separate the power for two circuits or you are adding a reverse module or power district. In terms of keeping things simple for the GCR build, we opted to go with the full metal rail joiner process.

To make these points work, Peco has isolated 15mm of the 'V' of the point completely from

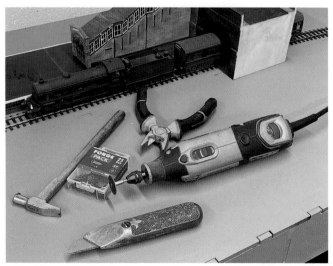

Tools of the trade for trackwork – a minidrill and cutting disc, pin hammer, pliers and craft knife.

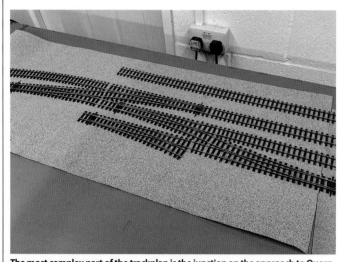

The most complex part of the trackplan is the junction on the approach to Quorn Magna. It has been built entirely with Peco large radius left and right hand bullhead rail points.

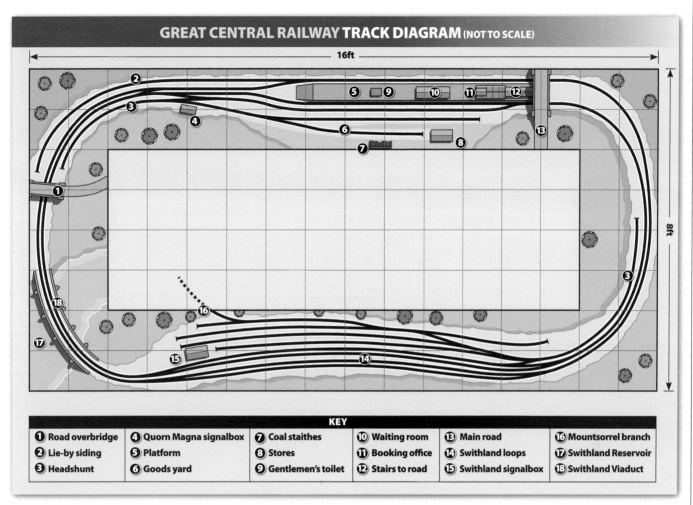

**GREAT CENTRAL RAILWAY TRACK DIAGRAM** (NOT TO SCALE)

16ft

8ft

| KEY | | | | | |
|---|---|---|---|---|---|
| ① Road overbridge | ④ Quorn Magna signalbox | ⑦ Coal staithes | ⑩ Waiting room | ⑬ Main road | ⑯ Mountsorrel branch |
| ② Lie-by siding | ⑤ Platform | ⑧ Stores | ⑪ Booking office | ⑭ Swithland loops | ⑰ Swithland Reservoir |
| ③ Headshunt | ⑥ Goods yard | ⑨ Gentlemen's toilet | ⑫ Stairs to road | ⑮ Swithland signalbox | ⑱ Swithland Viaduct |

the running lines. This is pre-soldered to a dropper wire which can be fed through a hole in the baseboard, but for those eager to get trains running you don't need to connect it right away to make the points operational. Just add the power feed to the layout and the majority of locomotives will run straight over the short dead section. Short wheelbase locomotives will be most at risk of stalling, but this can be easily remedied by adding a frog switch to a point motor or, for DCC, using a DCC Concepts Cobalt IP point

motor which has frog switching built in to its circuit board.

The tools required are identical to other types of track – we used a mini drill with a cutting disc to cut the rails to length, a craft knife to remove sleepers where necessary and cut cork sheeting to size and pliers to adjust rails into position. Our track was held in place using Peco ST280 track pins while the track was laid on top of Gaugemaster $^{1}/_{16}$ in thick cork. The only downside to our choice of cork was that the platform sections from Bachmann meant we needed

a double layer to bring the track to the right height for passengers to alight at Quorn Magna.

Baseboards joins were prepared by removing sleepers from the Peco track and adding in DCC Concepts 1.6mm thick pre-etched sleepers. Two 1.5mm pin holes were drilled in each of these sleepers so they could be fixed to the board surface with track pins, after which the sleepers were soldered to the rails to provide a fixing point for the rail ends at each baseboard joint. If you are building a permanent layout,

you won't need to add these additional sleepers to your track.

The most complex part of the trackplan so far is the junction on the approach to Quorn Magna station. This accommodates a crossover between the inner and outer circuits, spreads the main lines to go around the island platform, a link into the goods loop and point from the headshunt into the goods yard. It took a few goes to get the points in the right order to fit around the requirements of the plan and the baseboard framework, but »

An overview of the layout during construction. Quorn Magna is nearest the camera while Swithland Sidings is the far side.

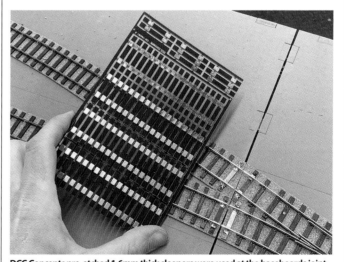

DCC Concepts pre-etched 1.6mm thick sleepers were used at the baseboards joint to hold the track in place for this portable layout. When dismantled the track will be retained in position by these sleepers as the rail ends are soldered to them.

**BUILDING THE GREAT CENTRAL RAILWAY**

A close up of one of the curved baseboard joints. More pre-etched sleepers are used for these curved board joint crossings and the track will be cut at an angle to match the position of the joint.

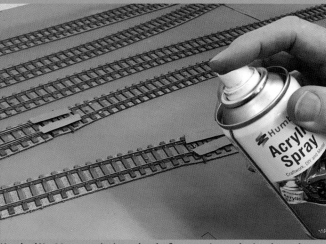

Humbrol No. 29 spray paint is used as the first stage in weathering the track. This tones down the sleepers and rail sides in one hit ready for ballasting.

we got there in the end. Working round the baseboard frame was the trickiest part, but essential to ensure we could add point motors underneath in the future.

We completed the full circuit of track for the layout straightaway, although there is further pointwork to be added to the Swithland Sidings side in the future. Next we moved on to add wire droppers

to all baseboards as required so that the full layout could be powered by DCC using the Gaugemaster Prodigy Advance system. The droppers, added using 7/0.2 equipment wire (seven strands of 0.2mm wire inside the insulation), were taken back to plug in terminal blocks underneath the layout for connection to the main power bus which feeds

power around the layout.

Having completed the basics of the wiring, we now had a working railway which we could test thoroughly before moving onto the scenic stages of the project.

### The start of scenery

Train running complete, we cleared the layout down again ready for the start of scenic work. The first task

was basic weathering of the track using Humbrol No. 29 in an aerosol spray can. This Dark Earth colour is an ideal base medium for track weathering and by covering the point blades with Tamiya masking tape we quickly added a coat of No. 29 across the entire track formation (after removing any buildings and structures) which was then left to dry.

The platform sections were then

Thompson 'B1' 4-6-0 61138 approaches the station with a passenger working and passes the scratchbuilt signalbox built by Paul Chapman for the layout. 'O4' 63598 is held at the signal while its crew prepares for departure.

The Bachmann Scenecraft platform sections were glued in place with Gorilla Contact Adhesive.

Ballast is a combination of Woodland Scenics fine and medium grade blended grey products. Here it is waiting to be glued down with diluted PVA adhesive.

glued in place with Gorilla Contact Adhesive and the area around the goods sidings was painted with Green Scene General Muck textured paint to provide the basis for road access to the railway yard. This all set the scene for ballasting of the layout using Woodland Scenics fine and medium grade blended grey ballast. The ballast has been glued in place with PVA glue let down to a 50:50 ratio with water. In a change to our usual practice, we added Isopropyl Alcohol to remove the surface tension from the water and aid the flow of glue into the ballast. The ballast was then wetted with water from a water mister before application of glue via a syringe.

Ballasting done, we moved onto another new method for our layout projects – expanding foam scenery. Traditionally we have used polystyrene blocks or card formers for the basis of landscaping but, partly enforced by a tight project deadline, we chose expanding foam for its quick drying times and inbuilt adhesive capabilities. It worked well, but we have a few tips if you are planning on using this method. First, you will need shuttering around the edge of your layout to contain the foam during application and setting. Secondly, expanding foam really does expand! We actually added too much in places which meant that it didn't fully set in the middle – using less would have cured this. Allied to the less is more approach, it is also important to build up the foam in layers rather than piling it on in one go. The total cost of the expanding foam method was less than £30 as »

Expanding foam has been used as the medium to create the landscape around the railway. Invert the can during spraying for the best performance and work in layers.

Once the foam has expanded you will find it is much larger than when first added to the layout. It needs carving back using a saw or hot wire foam cutter to create the final shape.

we used six cans to produce the scenic landform for Quorn Magna.

Having allowed it to expand and set overnight, we carved the landscape to its final shape using a combination of a hot wire cutter and a handsaw. The latter makes light work and less mess than with a material like polystyrene which tends to crumble when sawn.

As a final step to the landscaping process, we overlaid the carved foam with masking tape and layers of paper glued in place with neat PVA glue. This created a smooth hard shell on which we could start the landscaping process.

### Adding colour

To take away another step in the build process, our white paper hillsides were painted with PVA glue to which we added brown poster paint.

This glue application was used to hold the first layer of ground cover in place at the same time as colouring the landscape

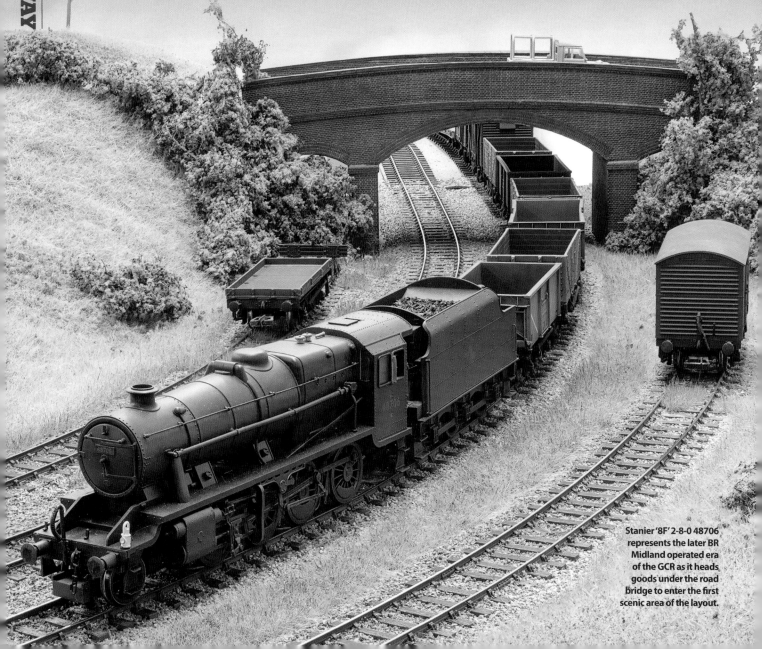

Stanier '8F' 2-8-0 48706 represents the later BR Midland operated era of the GCR as it heads goods under the road bridge to enter the first scenic area of the layout.

Having created the landscape shape from the expanding foam, the contours were covered with masking tape then overlaid with layers of paper coated with PVA for a quick and cheap method.

Quorn Magna's scratchbuilt signalbox, built specially for the layout by Paul Chapman, is bedded into the scenery with Woodland Scenics fine cinder ballast.

underneath and it worked a treat. Woodland Scenics fine blended green and blended earth turfs were sprinkled over the top of the wet brown PVA glue and allowed to dry before collecting the excess leaving the way clear for the first layers of static grass.

Our choice of grasses is Green Scene's summer, spring and straw colours which were loaded into a Noch Grasmaster in varying quantities for each application around the layout. This ensures that the grass textures don't become too repetitive. Further layers of static grass were applied using War World Scenics Layering Spray to build up the effect of the grasses and add further depth and texture.

That all brings us to the most enjoyable part of layout construction – scenic detailing,

where the bare landscape takes on a much more detailed and appealing finish. Our choice of material here is Woodland Scenics fine leaf foliage – a product we couldn't be without – combined with Primo Trees products for the larger trees around the layout. We added further layers of fine and coarse turf into the static grasses together with Woodland Scenics coloured pollen to suggest flower heads in the fields of green.

Quorn Magna is far from finished to the final standard that we want, but this really is only the beginning for the layout. Join us on pages 96-103 when we go into detail about the locomotives and rolling stock for the layout and look out for future features on Quorn Magna and Swithland Sidings in *Hornby Magazine* and on *KeyModelWorld.com*. ∎

Join us on pages 96-103

| USEFUL LINKS | |
| --- | --- |
| **Woodland Scenics** | www.bachmann.co.uk |
| **Green Scene** | www.green-scenes.co.uk |
| **Primo Trees** | www.primomodels.co.uk |
| **Bachmann Scenecraft** | www.bachmann.co.uk |
| **War World Scenics** | www.wwscenics.co.uk |
| **Hattons Model Railways** | www.hattons.co.uk |
| **The Model Tree Shop** | www.themodeltreeshop.co.uk |

| WHAT WE USED | | |
| --- | --- | --- |
| **PRODUCT** | **MANUFACTURER** | **CAT NO.** |
| GCR gentlemen's toilet | Scenecraft | 44-115A |
| GCR waiting room | Scenecraft | 44-116A |
| GCR booking office and canopy | Scenecraft | 44-117A |
| GCR high level station entrance | Scenecraft | 44-119A |
| GCR single track road bridge | Scenecraft | 44-121 |
| GCR island platform sections | Scenecraft | 44-153 |
| GCR island platform ramps | Scenecraft | 44-0008 |
| Weybourne road bridge | Scenecraft | 44-0072 |
| Peco code 75 bullhead track | Peco | SL-108F |
| Peco code 75 bullhead left-hand point | Peco | SLU-1188 |
| Peco code 75 bullhead right-hand point | Peco | SLU-1189 |
| Peco code 75 bullhead rail joiners | Peco | SL-114 |
| Peco code 75 bullhead buffer stops | Peco | SL-1140 |
| Fine blended green turf | Woodland Scenics | T1349 |
| Light green coarse turf | Woodland Scenics | T1363 |
| Burnt grass coarse turf | Woodland Scenics | T1362 |
| Light green fine leaf foliage | Woodland Scenics | F1132 |
| Medium green fine leaf foliage | Woodland Scenics | F1131 |
| Olive green fine leaf foliage | Woodland Scenics | F1133 |
| Purple pollen | Woodland Scenics | T4648 |
| Red pollen | Woodland Scenics | T4647 |
| Yellow pollen | Woodland Scenics | T4645 |
| Board fencing | Woodland Scenics | WA2892 |
| Long summer static grass | Green Scene | |
| Medium summer static grass | Green Scene | |
| Long spring static grass | Green Scene | |
| Medium spring static grass | Green Scene | |
| Long straw static grass | Green Scene | |
| Bushes, Type A, medium green | The Model Tree Shop | WB-SAMG |
| Bushes, Type B, olive green | The Model Tree Shop | WB-SBOL |
| Bushes, Type D, orange | The Model Tree Shop | WB-SDO |

Fencing on the layout is the new Woodland Scenics board fencing (WA2892). This superb new addition is pre-painted and comes with mounting pins for easy installation. To suit our scene we cut a couple of boards off and laid them up against the fence.

Static grass layers were built up and accented with Woodland Scenics fine and coarse turfs in blended green and light green colours respectively. Woodland Scenics purple and yellow pollen colours were added too together with a handful of Primo trees to decorate the scenery.

# Masterpieces in the GALLERY

We present a selection of the best layouts and model photography from the past year in *Hornby Magazine*.

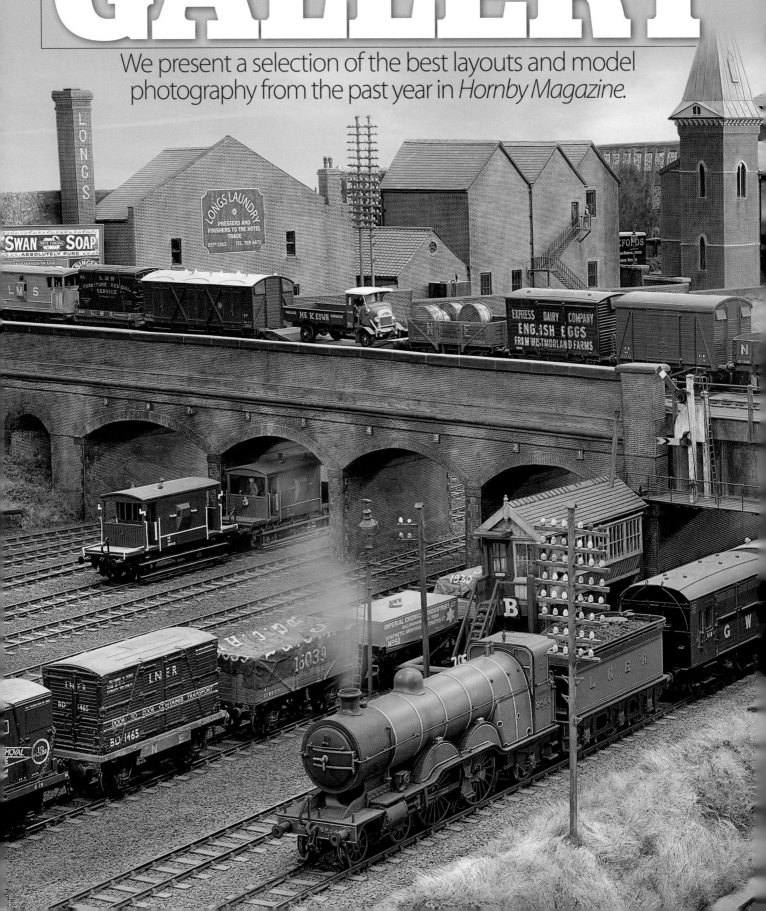

The Gresley Beat is a stunning portrayal of the London North Eastern Railway in North London in the 1930s, modelled in 'OO' gauge. An LMS 'Jinty' 0-6-0T crosses the bridge carrying the North London Line as an Ivatt 'Atlantic' passes below with a horsebox special and a Gresley 'A4' thumps along the lower main line with an express. Cliff Parsons' Gresley Beat featured in HM160. *Trevor Jones/Hornby Magazine.*

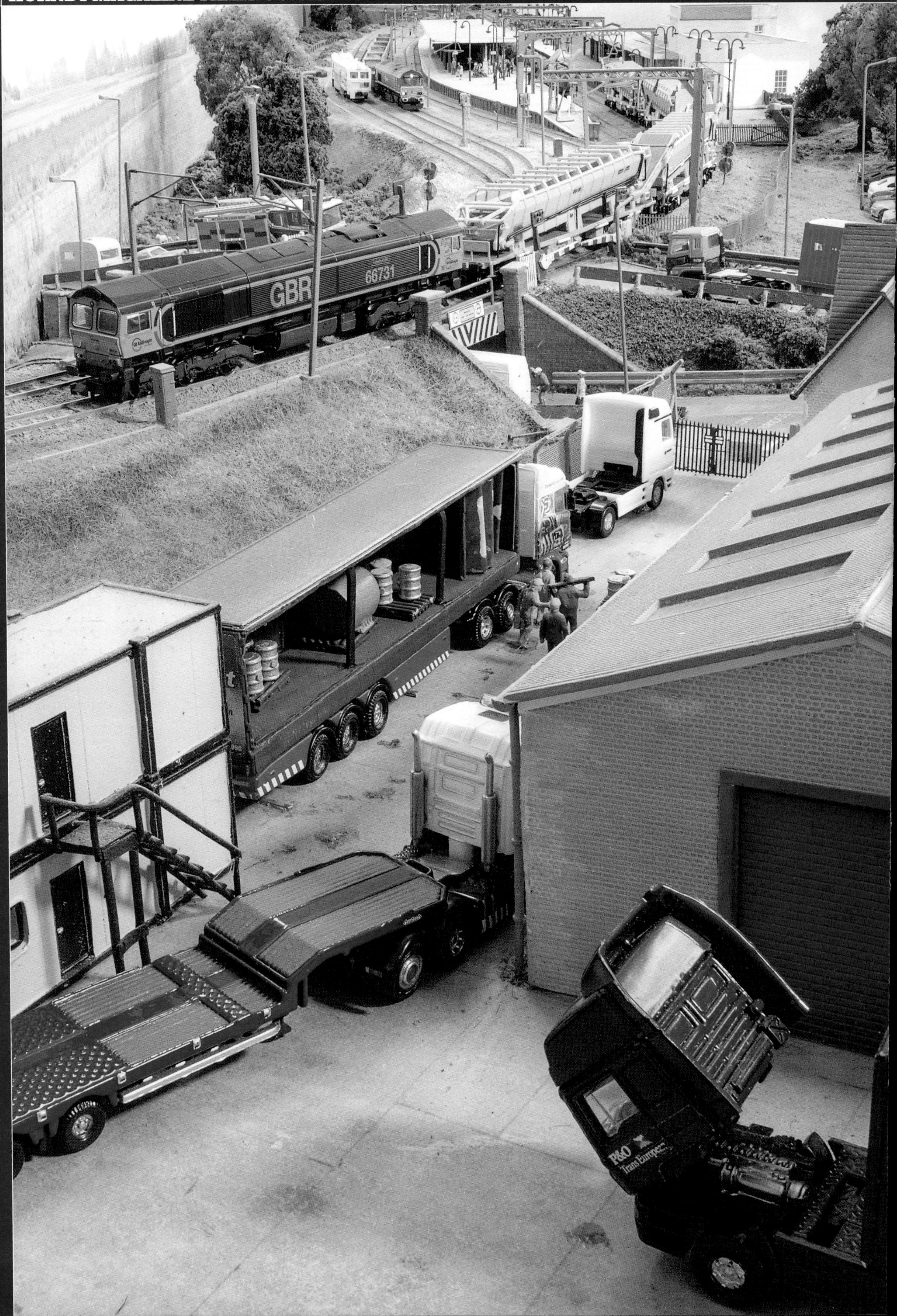
GBR
66731
P&O
Trans Europe

Above: It's rare that we showcase overseas layouts in *Hornby Magazine*, but for Gordon and Maggie Gravett's stunning 1:50 scale French metre gauge we made an exception. This outstanding piece of railway modelling is an inspiration to all and captures a typical rural French scene from the 1950s. Pempoul featured in HM157. Trevor Jones/*Hornby Magazine*.

Left: Neely takes close inspiration from Ely in Cambridge and is set in the modern era. The 'N' gauge layout is now owned by Scunthorpe Modern Image Group, having originally been built by Terry Metcalfe. A GBRf Class 66/7 departs with a 3D printed High Output Ballast Cleaner and passes the road haulage yard. Neely featured in HM158. Mike Wild/*Hornby Magazine*.

Below: Theobald's Yard is Orpington and District Model Railway Society's multi-gauge 7mm scale layout. It features narrow gauge operations inter-woven with standard gauge trains with a superb industrial backdrop. Here an 0-4-0VBT shunts wagons from one of the sidings while 4wDM collects stock from another. Theobald's Yard featured in HM158. Trevor Jones/*Hornby Magazine*.

Above: **Newpool-on-Trent is Graham Taylor's characterful home based 'OO' gauge layout. This inspirational railway system has three stations, gradients, a large locomotive depot and an off-scene 17 track storage yard in its armoury. A Stanier 'Duchess' rounds the curve to the station and passes the ashplant outside the main depot while a Garratt and Crosti '9F' receive attention from their crews. Newpool-on-Trent featured in HM161.** Mike Wild/*Hornby Magazine.*

Left: **Wimborne is the work of Wimborne Railway Society in 'OO' and models the Southern Region station as it was in the 1960s when steam still reigned supreme on the region. A Drummond '700' 0-6-0 is about to depart with a milk train as an 'M7' 0-4-4T draws into the platforms with a push-pull working. Wimborne featured in HM153.** Trevor Jones/*Hornby Magazine.*

Below: **Cornwallis Yard is set firmly in Great Western Railway territory around Plymouth in 1935 and 1936. A Collett 'Hall' 4-6-0 departs the high level station with a through working while a '1361' 0-6-0ST shunts in the yard. This 'EM' gauge layout featured in HM152.** Trevor Jones/*Hornby Magazine.*

Chilcompton Tunnel is a famous location on the former Somerset and Dorset Railway between Bath Green Park and Bournemouth and it has been recreated in 'OO' gauge by Steve Jones. A Stanier '8F' 2-8-0 has just emerged from the twin-bore tunnel as a Fowler '3F' 0-6-0 and '7F' 2-8-0 slog up grade with a second coal working destined for Bath Green Park and beyond. Chilcompton Tunnel featured in HM150.
Trevor Jones/*Hornby Magazine.*

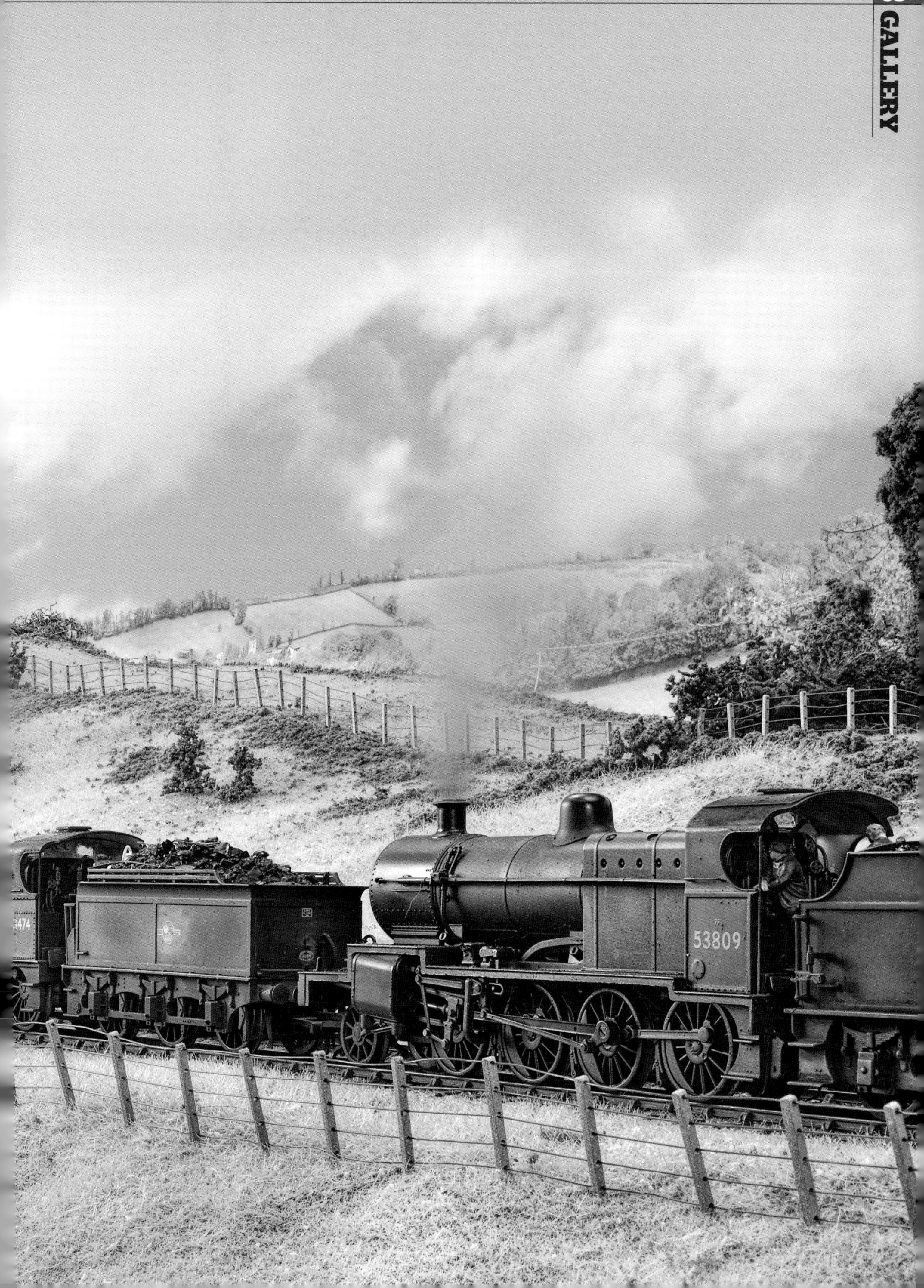
53809

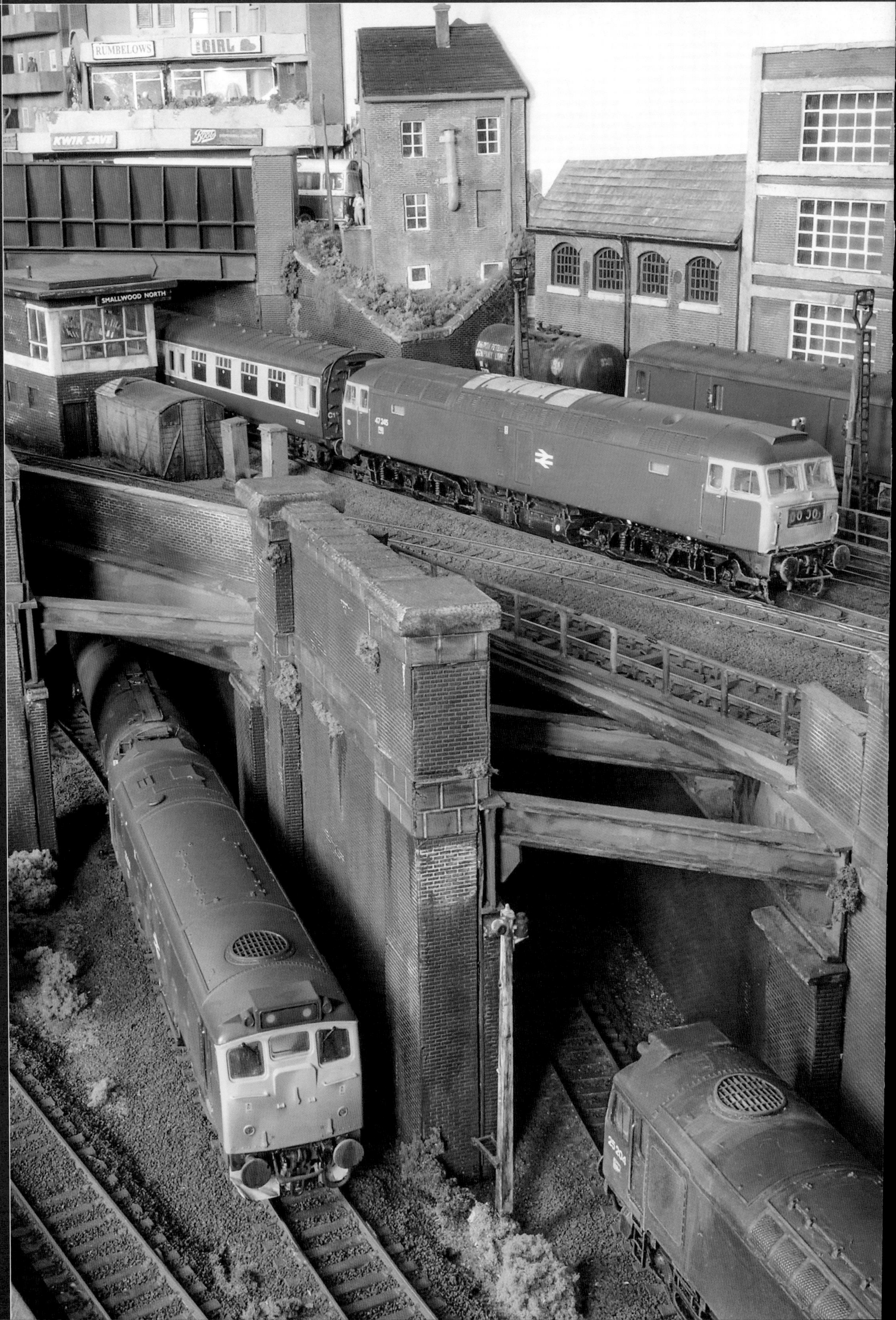
RUMBELOWS
GIRL
KWIK SAVE
SMALLWOOD NORTH

Above: **Fenny Stratford was a once busy station on the Varsity Line which linked the university cities of Oxford and Cambridge. Its location was chosen by builders David Court and Peter Ellis for its close proximity to their Milton Keynes homes. A Fowler '4F' 0-6-0 crosses the canal with a coal working as a BR '2MT' 2-6-0 heads in the opposite direction with a van train. Fenny Stratford featured in HM159.** Mike Wild/*Hornby Magazine*.

Left: **The Redditch Model Railway Club's latest 'OO' gauge layout is Smallwood – a 1970s era multi-level layout set in the West Midlands. A Class 47 heads a passenger working past the signalbox on the approach to the terminus station while Class 25s pass below in the exchange sidings for local industry. Smallwood featured in HM151.** Mike Wild/*Hornby Magazine*.

Below: **Brinklow is on the Trent Valley section of the West Coast Main Line and the Milton Keynes Model Railway Society choose this busy through station as the location for its latest 'N' gauge project. A Stanier 'Jubilee' steams along the Up fast with a milk working running alongside the Oxford Canal. Brinklow featured in HM151.** Mike Wild/*Hornby Magazine*.

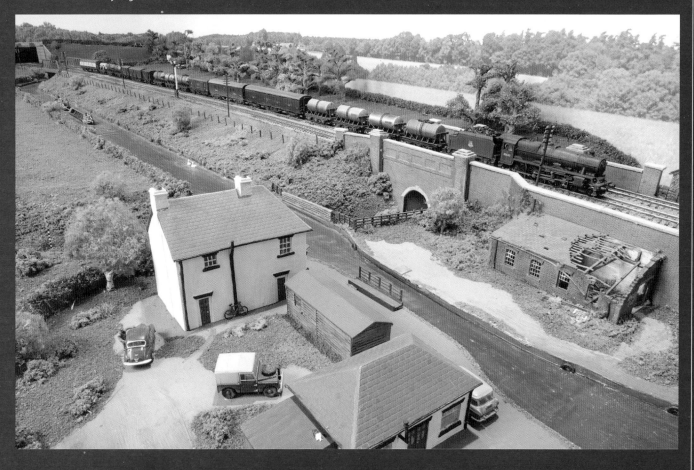

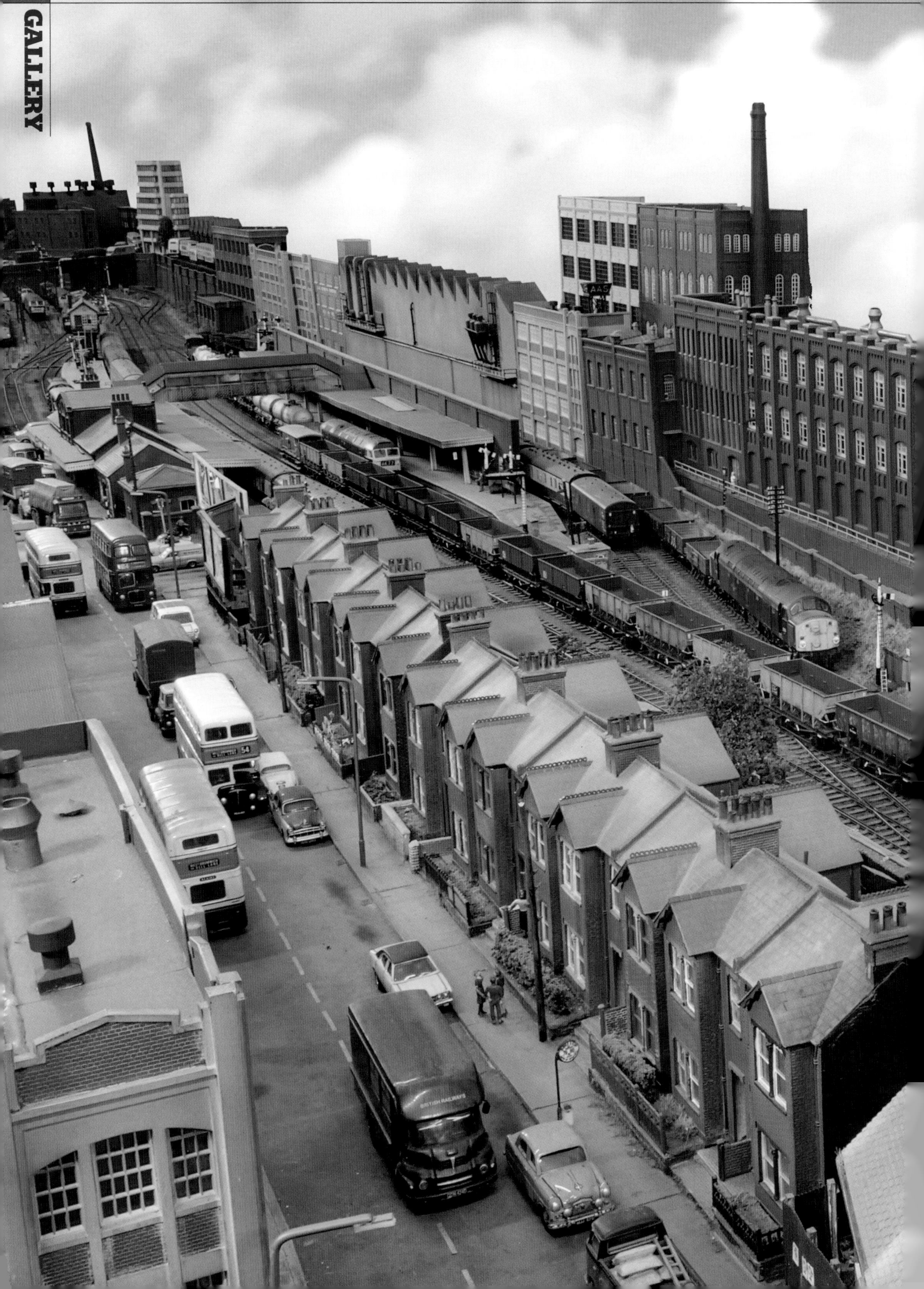

Greg Brookes' Shenston Road is an outstanding 'EM' gauge layout set in the West Midlands in the final years of the 1960s and early 1970s prior to the introduction of TOPS numbering. It features superbly detailed lineside and street scenes as well as locomotive and rolling stock weathering to the highest standard by Greg. A Class 35 'Hymek' leads empty 21ton coal hoppers through the station after making their way along the steel works branch. Shenston Road featured in HM154.
*Mike Wild/Hornby Magazine.*

# *Review of the Year*
# 2019-2020

*It has been a busy and challenging 12 months for manufacturers with a raft of new locomotive, carriage and wagon projects coming to fruition in 'OO', 'N' and 'O' gauges, despite global events disrupting production plans.* **MARK CHIVERS** *reflects on the past year's highlights.*

Right: **Pressed Steel DMUs were in vogue at Bachmann with the arrival of the Class 117 three-car and Class 121 single-car units for 'OO' gauge. It also delivered its 'OO' Class 158/159 diesel units as well as the Class 414 2-HAP for Southern Region modellers.**

Below: **Hornby's all-new Stanier 'Princess Royal' 4-6-2 arrived early in 2020 and a second round of releases came in early October too. Here 46207 *Princess Arthur of Connaught* crosses Topley Dale Viaduct with an express working.**

# 2020 HAS BEEN A FRAUGHT YEAR

for the whole world, and that has inevitably had an effect on railway modelling. The year started with immense promise as Hornby unveiled ambitious plans to celebrate its centenary and Bachmann introduced a new quarterly programme of announcements and releases.

However, by March the global pandemic looked to have disrupted worldwide manufacture and distribution of products. That said, despite some delays and setbacks, project development work continued and production has resumed, with a steady stream of new releases appearing with retailers. Bachmann even launched a new brand – EFE Rail – in August, with much of the new range ready to go shortly after.

Amazingly, 56 new or upgraded projects have been released during the past 12 months with 32 'OO', one 'OO9', 11 'N' and 12 'O' gauge projects making it to market. 21 new 'OO' gauge locomotives have appeared, with Bachmann back to form and issuing six new models, closely followed by Hornby with five new 'OO' locomotives. Dapol's 'OO' motive power roster was bolstered with four new arrivals. Heljan delivered five 'O' gauge locomotives of its own, together with two new 'O' gauge examples on behalf of Hattons Originals, plus two upgraded 'OO' engines, while Dapol added two new 'O' gauge locomotives and two 'O' gauge wagons. Bachmann upgraded its 'N' gauge Class 70/8 Co-Co diesel and EFE Rail launched with a new 'N' gauge diesel and upgraded 'OO' gauge steam locomotive.

In terms of rolling stock,

Bachmann completed three new 'N' gauge and two 'OO' gauge projects, while Hornby concluded three new 'OO' gauge models. Smaller manufacturers made up the remainder with Revolution Trains delivering three new 'N' gauge wagons, Accurascale with one new 'OO' gauge wagon, Irish Railway Models with two new 'OO' wagon projects and Cavalex Models with one new 'OO' wagon. C=Rail and sister company Realtrack Models each delivered a new 'N' gauge wagon, Oxford Rail added another 'OO' gauge wagon to its range, Rails of Sheffield delivered its 3D printed 'OO' gauge SECR 10ton box van, Minerva Models released its 'O' gauge GWR five plank open wagon and Peco completed its 'OO9' Ffestiniog Railway 'Bug Box' coaches. In all, 33 new locomotives, four new carriage and 19 new wagon projects appeared during the year – not bad, considering the backdrop. Inevitably, plans for forthcoming models have slipped a little, but indications are that there is plenty still to come before the year end.

## Locomotives

Bachmann delivered its all-new 'OO' gauge London and Northern Eastern Railway (LNER) 'J72' 0-6-2T just as *Hornby Magazine Yearbook No. 12* closed for press. Four versions of the 'J72' appeared in LNER black, BR black with early crests, BR black with late crests and NER lined green. Amongst its impressive new specification were a coreless motor, Next18 Digital Command Control (DCC) decoder socket, factory-fitted 15mm x 11mm speaker and firebox flicker. A new variant of the manufacturer's 'OO' gauge Class 24 – the headcode fitted Class 24/1 – arrived at the turn of the year. Its new headcode »

Bachmann launched the EFE Rail brand to the market in August 2020 which included former DJ Models products which are owned by Kernow Model Rail Centre. Amongst those is the Hunslet 'Austerity' 0-6-0ST for 'OO' gauge as well as the revival of the 'N' gauge Class 17.

| TABLE 1 – 2019-2020 NEW READY-TO-RUN LOCOMOTIVES | | | | |
|---|---|---|---|---|
| **MODEL** | **SCALE** | **MANUFACTURER** | **RELEASED** | **FEATURED** |
| LNER 'J72' 0-6-0T | 'OO' | Bachmann | September 2019 | HM149 |
| Ruston and Hornsby 48DS 4wDM | 'OO' | Hornby | October 2019 | HM150 |
| LNER 'A3' 4-6-2 | 'O' | Hattons | November 2019 | HM151 |
| BR Class 50 Co-Co diesel | 'O' | Heljan | December 2019 | HM152 |
| Class 66 Co-Co diesel | 'OO' | Hattons | December 2019 | HM152 |
| Sentinel 'Y1'/'Y3' 4wVBT | 'O' | Dapol | December 2019 | HM152 |
| BR Class 158/159 Diesel Multiple Unit | 'OO' | Bachmann | January 2020 | HM153 |
| BR Class 24/1 Bo-Bo diesel | 'OO' | Bachmann | January 2020 | HM153 |
| BR Class 21 Bo-Bo diesel | 'OO' | Dapol | January 2020 | HM153 |
| BR Class 33/0 Bo-Bo diesel | 'O' | Heljan | January 2020 | HM153 |
| BR Class 03 0-6-0DM shunter | 'O' | Heljan | January 2020 | HM153 |
| BR Class 27 Bo-Bo diesel (new variant) | 'OO' | Heljan | January 2020 | HM153 |
| BR Class 29 Bo-Bo diesel | 'OO' | Dapol | February 2020 | HM154 |
| LMS 'Princess Royal' 4-6-2 | 'OO' | Hornby | February 2020 | HM154 |
| GWR Parcels diesel railcar | 'OO' | Dapol | February 2020 | HM154 |
| L&MR Stephenson's *Rocket* 0-2-2 | 'OO' | Hornby | February 2020 | HM154 |
| BR Class 121 diesel railcar | 'OO' | Bachmann | March 2020 | HM155 |
| Class 70/8 Co-Co diesel (air intakes) | 'N' | Graham Farish | March 2020 | HM155 |
| BR Class 35 'Hymek' B-B diesel-hydraulic | 'O' | Heljan | March 2020 | HM155 |
| GWR '14XX' 0-4-2T | 'O' | Dapol | April 2020 | HM156 |
| LBSCR 'Terrier' 0-6-0T | 'OO' | Rails of Sheffield/Dapol | May 2020 | HM157 |
| LNER 'A4' 4-6-2 | 'O' | Hattons | May 2020 | HM157 |
| BR Class 33/0 Bo-Bo diesel (HI headlights) | 'OO' | Heljan | May 2020 | HM157 |
| BR Class 117 Diesel Multiple Unit | 'OO' | Bachmann | June 2020 | HM158 |
| GWR '5101'/'61XX' 2-6-2T | 'OO' | Hornby | June 2020 | HM158 |
| BR Class 24 Bo-Bo diesel (upgraded) | 'OO' | Sutton's Locomotive Works | June 2020 | HM158 |
| BR Class 37 Co-Co diesel (upgraded) | 'O' | Heljan | July 2020 | HM159 |
| LNER 'J94' 0-6-0ST | 'OO' | EFE Rail | August 2020 | HM160 |
| LMS 'Princess Coronation' 4-6-2 (Dublo) | 'OO' | Hornby | August 2020 | HM160 |
| LSWR '0330' 0-6-0ST | 'OO' | OO Works | August 2020 | HM160 |
| BR Class 17 Bo-Bo diesel | 'N' | EFE Rail | August 2020 | HM160 |
| BR Class 414 2-HAP Electric Multiple Unit | 'OO' | Bachmann | September 2020 | HM161 |
| BR Class 252 High Speed Train – Prototype | 'N' | Dapol | September 2020 | HM161 |

boxes emitted a realistic yellow glow on test, while its detailing included superb underframe pipework, separately fitted lamp irons, bufferbeam parts and more.

During January, the first of Bachmann's new 'OO' gauge Class 158/159 Diesel Multiple Units (DMU) was received for review, our sample appearing in three-car Class 159 form in Network SouthEast colours. Again, this new release was brimming with technology including factory-fitted digital sound and cube speakers, illuminated destination blinds, PluX22 DCC decoder socket and working BSI couplers to the outer ends. Interestingly, multiple units were a common theme this year with Bachmann's 'OO' Class 121 diesel railcar appearing during March, capturing the distinctive appearance of these Pressed Steel single car units. Our review sample was finished in BR blue and grey with Newquay and Par destination blinds, while other colour schemes included BR green with small yellow warning panels, revised BR Network SouthEast and BR chocolate and cream, the latter model a limited edition example for Kernow Model Rail Centre (KMRC).

During June, Bachmann's 'OO'

gauge three-car Class 117 DMU appeared, replicating the type accurately in ready-to-run form for the first time with Driving Motor Brake Second (DMBS), Trailer Composite with Lavatory (TCL) and Driving Motor Second (DMS) vehicles. Tooling differences were incorporated across the releases, appearing with or without corridor connections, different exhaust styles and more. Finally, on the multiple unit front, Bachmann's long-awaited 'OO' gauge 2-HAP two-car Electric Multiple Unit (EMU) arrived for review during September. Our sample was finished as unit 6061 in BR plain green and featured a 21-pin DCC decoder socket, headcode illumination and interior lights.

Hornby's delightful 'OO' gauge Ruston and Hornsby 48DS 4wDM diesel shunter arrived in the *Hornby Magazine* office for review during October 2019. It came with a semi-permanently coupled Conflat wagon to aid power collection, three-pole motor and six-pin DCC decoder socket.

Meanwhile, with the centenary celebrations under way and trade shows in full swing, February 2020 proved a busy month for the Margate based manufacturer as it delivered the first issue of its all-new 'OO' gauge Stephenson's *Rocket* 0-2-2 train pack containing three coaches – *Despatch, Experience* and *Times* – in Liverpool & Manchester

Railway yellow and black. This outstanding release appeared in Tri-ang branded packaging as part of Hornby's special Centenary range. A standard model in Railway Museum branded packaging appeared a few months later with three different carriages – *Globe, Renown* and *Wellington*. Also appearing during the month was its new 'OO' Stanier

'Princess Royal' 4-6-2 with firebox glow, five-pole motor, flywheel and fully decorated cab interior. Our review sample was finished as 6201 *Princess Elizabeth* in LMS maroon with Stanier 4,000gallon tender.

The first of Hornby's newly tooled Great Western Railway (GWR) 'Large Prairie' 2-6-2Ts appeared during June, boasting a five-pole motor,

8-pin DCC decoder socket, sprung metal buffers and impressive detailing throughout. Rounding off Hornby's 'OO' gauge locomotive projects, August saw the eagerly awaited *very* limited edition Stanier 'Princess Coronation' 4-6-2 arrive on retailers' shelves. It differed from Hornby's standard high-fidelity model in that the locomotive »

A highlight in Bachmann's product releases was its 45ton Ransomes and Rapier steam crane for 'OO' gauge. The finely detailed model features a poseable jib, working cables, pistons and a full cab interior too. Here it takes care of a recovery job at Twelve Trees Junction.

Heljan's 'O' gauge Class 50 was an instant hit on arrival in December with the most popular versions selling out almost immediately – so much so that a second production is planned for release in 2021. The BR 'large logo' version, numbered 50049 *Defiance* in the *Hornby Magazine* workshop, poses on shed at Seven Mill Depot.

body was diecast metal, emulating the original model produced by Hornby Dublo in 1947. Supplied in special 'candy-stripe' packaging, just 500 models were issued.

Dapol also enjoyed a busy year of locomotive releases with four new 'OO' locomotive projects coming to fruition. First up was the original North British Type 2 (BR Class 21) Bo-Bo diesel with disc headcodes during January. Weighing in at almost 500g, it featured a five-

pole motor, twin brass flywheels, all-wheel drive and see-through etched bodyside and roof grilles. The following month saw the Class 29 variant released, with clear detail differences between it and the Class 21 such as sealed communication doors, central headcode, revised windscreen wiper positions, roof differences and more.

Dapol's NBL Type 2s were closely followed by the 'OO' gauge GWR Parcels Railcar, finished as unique

railcar W17W in BR crimson with Express Parcels branding. Allied to its diecast chassis was an all-new body moulding with separately fitted roof conduit, door handrails, stub buffers and a bespoke interior moulding with racking. The manufacturer's fourth 'OO' gauge arrival of the year was a collaboration with Rails of Sheffield and the National Railway Museum – the Stroudley 'Terrier' 0-6-0T. Bristling with detail, the models feature firebox glow, factory-

fitted 'cube' speaker, five-pole motor and Next 18 DCC decoder socket.

Talking of retailer exclusive models, Hattons Originals delivered its all-new 'OO' gauge Class 66 Co-Co diesel for review towards the end of 2019 ahead of the first batch arriving in early 2020. 32 different models were initially announced, with further high-profile examples added to the release schedule. Highlights include heavy diecast chassis, five-pole motor, twin

Hornby's 2020 releases weren't just focused on high-profile locomotives, as it produced an all-new GWR 'Large Prairie' 2-6-2T in '5101' and '61XX' forms. Here 6145 leads a rake of Collett bow-end non-corridor stock through the junction on Topley Dale.

Modern traction modellers received a brand-new Class 66 for 'OO' gauge – and Hattons produced over 30 versions too! 66088 demonstrates DB branded ex-EWS maroon and gold as its exits the tunnel on Topley Dale with a cement train.

flywheels, 21-pin DCC decoder socket, etched metal grilles, rotating axle covers and exposed pipework.

Heljan's 'OO' gauge Class 27 reappeared during February, this time with sealed cab fronts, sliding cab windows and tablet catcher recesses beneath the driver's windows, a combination of tooling which had not previously been offered. Similarly, the manufacturer's 'OO' gauge revised Class 33/0 resurfaced with retailers in May, this time with high-intensity cab front headlights for the first time on this version of the tooling, another welcome addition which opened up further livery options.

Sutton's Locomotive Works' previously released high-fidelity 'OO' gauge Class 24 Bo-Bo diesel appeared during the year in a series of new guises, sporting enhancements to detailing and its onboard digital sound file. Meanwhile, low-volume manufacturer OO Works also delivered another 'OO' gauge ready-to-run project in August with the release of its London & South Western Railway (LSWR) '0330' 0-6-0ST. Our review model of the all-metal hand-assembled 'Saddleback' was finished as No. 4 in Kent & East Sussex lined green. Detailing included metal handrails, lamp irons, copper pipework and a coreless motor.

Last but by no means least in terms of 'OO' gauge locomotive releases this year, EFE Rail launched amid a blaze of publicity from parent company Bachmann with a reworked LNER 'J94' 0-6-0ST amongst the releases. Formerly developed by DJ Models, the locomotive now bears Kernow Model Rail Centre (KMRC) branding to the underside of the chassis and has been upgraded with a revised motor and neater Next 18 DCC decoder socket arrangement.

Looking to 'N' gauge, two new locomotive projects and a tooling upgrade were completed during the year with EFE Rail's new Class 17 Bo-Bo diesel, Dapol's BR Class 252 High Speed Train – Prototype (HST-P) and Graham Farish's Class 70/8 Co-Co diesel. EFE Rail's all-new 'N' gauge locomotive was also originally a DJ Models project which has subsequently transferred to KMRC and been released through Bachmann's new model railway brand. It features a coreless motor, Next 18 DCC decoder socket, all-wheel drive and directional head and taillights.

Dapol's exclusive 'N' gauge prototype HST arrived during September. Originally only available to pre-order through the company's website, two variants of the newly tooled power cars have been produced in original passenger

and departmental liveries. Newly tooled Trailer First (TF) and Trailer Second (TS) saloons have also been manufactured, while a pair of catering cars based on existing Mk 3 buffet tooling have also been offered in the HST-P colour scheme. The new TF/TS coaches correctly feature recessed door handles, locomotive-hauled roof configuration and buffers, while the HST-P motorised power car features all-wheel drive, Next18 DCC decoder socket and directional lighting. In terms of upgrades to tooling, Bachmann's 'N' gauge Class 70/8 Co-Co diesel received new air intake detailing and tweaks to better reflect the present-day prototypes.

The popularity of 'O' gauge continues apace with nine new or upgraded 7mm scale ready-to-run locomotives appearing this year. Of these, seven were Heljan developments while two were Dapol projects. Heljan delivered five of its own 'O' gauge locomotives, together with two commissions for Hattons Originals. First to appear was Hattons' Gresley 'A3' 4-6-2 during November. First announced in 2016, the Heljan-produced model features a five-pole motor, brass flywheel and a wealth of separately fitted detailing. The model's tooling suite covers both LNER and BR period prototypes with corridor/non-corridor tenders, choice of chimneys and domes, 'German' smoke deflector options and more.

Heljan also delivered its eagerly-awaited 'O' gauge model of the English Electric Class 50 Co-Co diesel during December 2019 with an impressive selection of liveries including BR blue, BR 'large logo'

blue, original and revised Network SouthEast in unnumbered format, while fully-finished models were also offered as 50007 *Sir Edward Elgar* in GWR lined green and 50149 *Defiance* in Railfreight Distribution triple grey plus two limited edition models for Hattons as railtour 'celebrities' 50008 *Thunderer* in Laira blue and 50015 *Valiant* in 'Dutch' grey and yellow.

2020 was heralded with the arrival of Heljan's improved 'O' gauge model of the BR Class 33 Bo-Bo diesel with new tooling for the body, bogies and an enhanced mechanism too. Now available with or without high-intensity headlights, it was also offered in a raft of liveries. The new specification included improved roof profile, modified exhaust ports and colour-coded wiring to aid DCC installation.

January also witnessed the release of Heljan's 'O' gauge BR Class 03 diesel shunter. Another eagerly awaited model, it boasted a five-pole motor, flywheel, 21-pin DCC decoder socket, etched metal grilles and choice of conical or 'flower pot' chimneys.

In March, Heljan relaunched its debut 'O' gauge locomotive, the Western Region Class 35 'Hymek' B-B diesel hydraulic, 15 years on from its original release in 2005. The manufacturer took the opportunity to incorporate a few revisions to this latest version with new motors, colour-coded wiring, LED lighting, revised circuit board and a slight reduction to its overall weight to enhance it further.

In May, Heljan delivered its second 'O' gauge project for Hattons Originals with the visually »

| TABLE 2 – 2019-2020 NEW READY-TO-RUN CARRIAGES | | | | |
|---|---|---|---|---|
| MODEL | SCALE | MANUFACTURER | RELEASED | FEATURED |
| BR Mk 3 sliding door carriages | 'OO' | Hornby | May 2020 | HM157 |
| LNER Thompson carriages | 'N' | Bachmann (Graham Farish) | June 2020 | HM158 |
| Ffestiniog Railway 'Bug Box' coaches | 'OO9' | Peco | July 2020 | HM159 |
| BR Mk 2f carriages | 'N' | Bachmann (Graham Farish) | September 2020 | HM161 |

Left: **Hattons stepped up to 'O' gauge to create exclusive models of the Gresley 'A3' 4-6-2 and 'A4' 4-6-2 in conjunction with Heljan. Here Gresley 'A3' 60103** *Flying Scotsman* **poses on Seven Mill Depot.**

Below: **Accurascale has continued to impress with its highly detailed rolling stock releases including the PFA four-wheel container flats with 20ft containers. Class 37/7 37710 leads a rake of British Fuels liveried coal containers loaded onto PFA flats through Topley Dale station.**

| TABLE 3 – 2019-2020 NEW READY-TO-RUN WAGONS | | | | |
|---|---|---|---|---|
| MODEL | SCALE | MANUFACTURER | RELEASED | FEATURED |
| KQA pocket container wagon | 'N' | C=Rail | October 2019 | HM150 |
| SECR 10ton box van | 'OO' | Rails of Sheffield/Dapol | October 2019 | ------ |
| Ransomes and Rapier 45ton steam crane | 'OO' | Bachmann | November 2019 | HM151 |
| GWR five-plank open wagon | 'O' | Minerva Model Railways | January 2020 | ------ |
| PFA container flat wagon | 'OO' | Accurascale | January 2020 | HM153 |
| LSWR 24ton brake van | 'OO' | Hornby | January 2020 | HM153 |
| LMS 20ton brake van | 'OO' | Hornby | January 2020 | HM153 |
| PCA cement tank wagon | 'N' | Realtrack Models | January 2020 | HM153 |
| KFA container flat wagon | 'N' | Revolution Trains | January 2020 | HM153 |
| BR 'Sturgeon' bogie rail flat wagon | 'N' | Revolution Trains | January 2020 | ----- |
| HOA coal hopper wagon | 'N' | Revolution Trains | March 2020 | HM155 |
| CIE bogie fertiliser wagon | 'OO' | Irish Railway Models | April 2020 | HM156 |
| 8ton banana box van | 'O' | Dapol | April 2020 | HM156 |
| HKA bogie hopper wagon | 'OO' | Bachmann | August 2020 | HM160 |
| HKA bogie hopper wagon | 'N' | Bachmann (Graham Farish) | August 2020 | HM160 |
| BR 'Turbot' bogie spoil wagon | 'O' | Dapol | August 2020 | HM160 |
| BBA/BLA bogie steel carrier | 'OO' | Cavalex Models | September 2020 | HM160 |
| 12ton tank wagon | 'OO' | Oxford Rail | September 2020 | HM160 |
| CIE 42ft bogie flat wagons (various) | 'OO' | Irish Railway Models | September 2020 | HM160 |

stunning Gresley 'A4' 4-6-2, offered with or without valances. Options also included single or double chimneys, corridor and non-corridor tenders and a wide selection of liveries including LNER silver, LNER garter blue, BR lined blue with early crests, BR lined green with early crests and BR lined green with late crests. July also saw the return of Heljan's original split headcode Class 37/0 for 'O' gauge using the original body tooling, but with an upgraded DCC friendly chassis which also incorporated LED lighting. The fuel tanks were also modified to meet the standard of more recent releases.

Both of Dapol's 'O' gauge locomotive projects during the year were petite by comparison but just as compelling, with the release of the Sentinel 'Y1/Y3' 4wVBT and GWR '14XX' 0-4-2T. The Sentinel appeared just before the end of 2019, with our review sample finished as 68164 in BR black with early crests. The impressive specification included a five-pole motor, flywheel, 21-pin DCC decoder socket, detailed cab interior, opening doors and sprung buffers. During April, production samples of Dapol's 'O' gauge GWR '14XX' 0-4-2T eventually touched down. We were lucky to have two opportunities to scrutinise the model – firstly a pre-production sample in HM150 and a final production sample of 1426 in BR lined green with late crests in HM156. It was certainly worth the wait.

*See Table 1 for the full list of new locomotives.*

## Carriages

With much emphasis on newly-tooled locomotives through the year, just four standalone carriage projects were completed with Bachmann delivering two new sets of 'N' gauge vehicles, Hornby debuting its 'OO' gauge sliding door BR Mk 3 carriages and Peco launched the first of their Ffestiniog Railway 'Bug Box' coaches for 'OO9'.

With the full-size railway adopting a programme of reworking a sizeable chunk of the BR Mk 3 fleet for use with CrossCountry, GWR and ScotRail, Hornby followed suit in May and released its newly-tooled 'OO' gauge sliding door vehicles, together with matching HST power cars. Seven different carriage types were tooled, including Trailer First Disabled (TFD), Trailer Composite Catering (TCC), Trailer Standard (TS), Trailer Standard Disabled (TSD), Trailer Standard Lavatory (TSL), Trailer Guard First Buffet (TGFB) and Trailer Guard Standard (TGS). Full sets of coaches in each operator's respective colour schemes were produced, enabling prototypical sets to be modelled.

Bachmann's new carriage releases were limited to its Graham Farish 'N' gauge range this year. In June, the manufacturer's 'N' gauge LNER Thompson coaches arrived with Corridor Brake Third (BTK), Corridor Composite (CK), Corridor First (FK) and Corridor Third (TK) vehicles issued in LNER faux teak and BR carmine and cream. Meanwhile, during September the first of Bachmann's new 'N' gauge BR Mk 2f carriages arrived for review with examples of an Open First (FO), Restaurant First Buffet (RFB) and Driving Brake Second Open (DBSO). An Open Brake Second (BSO) and

Open Second (TSO) complete the range. Delivery started in October.

Finally, Peco issued the first of its new 'OO9' Ffestiniog Railway carriages during the summer with First Class, Third Class and Open Third vehicles received for review. Nicknamed 'Bug Boxes', these delightful new coaches were well detailed and neatly decorated in Ffestiniog Railway green and cream livery.

*See Table 2 for the full list of new carriages.*

## Wagons and departmental stock

While the number of completed wagon and departmental projects wasn't quite as prolific as last year, there was still plenty to catch modellers' attention. Bachmann's release schedule for the year included two new 'OO' gauge rolling stock projects and the first of these was truly outstanding – the Ransomes and Rapier 45ton steam crane. Appearing just in time for Christmas, this stunning new release was issued in Southern Railway grey, Great Western grey, BR black with early crests and BR departmental red. Detailing was superb throughout, offering a level of finesse previously not seen on a ready-to-run 'OO' gauge

crane. The jib could be raised and lowered, turned through 360°, plus the crane also featured moving pistons, full brake rigging, carefully threaded pulley wheels and a fully detailed cab interior. For something altogether more modern, Bachmann's second 'OO' gauge release was the HKA high capacity hopper wagon. Our review sample was finished in DB Schenker red, while examples in original National Power livery were also offered.

For something a little different - certainly in terms of production methods - Rails of Sheffield took delivery of the first examples of its 'OO' gauge 3D printed South Eastern & Chatham Railway (SECR) 10ton box vans in SR brown, SR brown with BR lettering and BR grey in late 2019. Working in partnership with Dapol, it utilised new technology and proved very popular, the low-volume run selling-out on pre-order.

Hornby's new 'OO' gauge wagon releases also amounted to just two vehicles this year, with its LSWR and LMS brake vans appearing during January. Announced in 2019, the LSWR 'New Van' was the first of the type to appear from the manufacturer, while the LMS 20ton brake van replaced an older example in the range. »

January also saw Accurascale take delivery of its eagerly awaited PFA four-wheel container flat wagons. These highly detailed wagons were offered in multiple triple-packs containing individually numbered vehicles with a choice of full height 20ft open containers or low-height low level nuclear waste containers.

Oxford Rail also delivered just one new 'OO' gauge wagon project during the year with the release of its 12ton tank wagon in September. Our review sample was finished in Mobil black and featured a slender tank barrel, metal strapping and securing stays, fine filler cap and locking mechanism together with a well-detailed underframe.

September may also have witnessed a new benchmark in wagon modelling with Cavalex Models' new 'OO' gauge BBA bogie steel carrier wagons. It was the

second 'OO' wagon project for the manufacturer and featured a heavy diecast chassis, exquisite etched metal mesh decking, metal stanchions, outstanding bogie detailing from all angles, neatly formed underframe cable runs and more. A batch of BLA bogie steel coil wagons were also produced exclusively for Rails of Sheffield.

For Irish outline modellers, Irish Railway Models (IRM) delivered a selection of new wagons during the year. First arrivals were eight different fertiliser wagons in red oxide. Produced in twin sets, they featured neatly moulded doors, sprung buffers, rotating axle covers and fertiliser loads. These were followed shortly after with three very different wagons based on the same 42ft bogie flat wagon containing Guinness kegs, spoil containers and a rather colourful

three-vehicle weed spray train. Each utilised the diecast metal flat wagons as the basis, featured neatly moulded Sambre et Meuse bogies and delicate pipe runs.

2020 was certainly a good year for 'N' gauge modellers of the contemporary scene with seven new wagon projects appearing. Leading the field, Revolution Trains (RT) completed three of its crowd-funded 'N' gauge projects early in the year, with its Tiphook PFA/KFA bogie container flat wagon arriving for review in January. This wagon was offered with two different types of bogie, featured a diecast spine, plastic deck, metal detailing and variations to buffer styles and handwheel positions. January also witnessed the arrival of RT's new 'N' gauge 'Sturgeon' engineers' low deck bogie wagons. These distinctive vehicles were produced

with and without dropside doors in a range of liveries including BR black, BR gulf red, BR olive green, BR departmental yellow and BR 'Dutch' yellow and grey. For its third release of the year, RT's 'N' gauge high-capacity HOA bogie hopper wagon arrived for review in March. Five different livery options were offered in EWS Construction, DB Schenker, Cemex, Ermewa/Tarmac and VTG/Mendip Rail schemes, together with seven individually numbered wagons for each (one single wagon and two triple-packs per colour scheme).

C=Rail Intermodal delivered its 'N' gauge ready-to-run KQA pocket container wagon just as *Hornby Magazine Yearbook No. 12* closed for press last October, a perfect companion to the manufacturer's extensive range of 'N' gauge Intermodal containers. Three

Sutton's Locomotive Works evolved its outstanding Class 24/0 model for 4mm scale with upgrades to the body, glazing, details and sound profile. Here a trio of 2020 releases decorate the station approach at Topley Dale consisting of D5083 in BR green, 97201 in Railway Technical Centre red and blue and D5021 in BR Polyurethane blue with small yellow warning panels.

Dapol's 'OO' gauge range grew during the past year with products including the long-awaited Class 21/29 Type 2 diesels making their debut. Here Class 29 D6114 approaches the tunnel on Topley Dale and passes Class 21 D6120 in original condition.

models were released – one empty and two supplied with weighted 40ft 'High Cube' containers in OOCL grey and NYK Logistics blue. Meanwhile, C=Rail's sister company, Realtrack Models, also delivered its first 'N' gauge ready-to-run wagon project in January - the PCA bulk cement wagon. Manufactured on its behalf by Accurascale, the model utilised development data from the 'OO' gauge models released the previous year. This resulted in fine detailing to the crisply moulded hopper, ladders, etched walkways and superbly accomplished underframe.

Completing the year's 'N' gauge wagon projects, Bachmann delivered its new 'N' gauge HKA high-capacity bogie hopper in August. Interestingly, this project was completed at the same time as the company's 'OO' gauge example – possibly a first. It too featured a neatly moulded body profile, choice of National Power and DB Schenker liveries and turned metal wheels.

For 'O' gauge modellers it was a quieter year rolling stock wise, with just three wagon projects appearing during the period under review. At the turn of the year Minerva Model Railways took delivery of its 'O' gauge GWR five-plank open wagons in GWR grey and BR grey finishes, while during April Dapol's new 'O' gauge 8ton Banana box van arrived. Utilising the manufacturer's 10ft wheelbase chassis, our review samples were finished in early and late BR bauxite as vehicles 880989 and 881127, respectively. They featured full underframe detailing, compensation bar, brass bearings and turned metal wheels. Later in the year, Dapol delivered its 'O' gauge 'Turbot' bogie ballast/spoil wagon during August. Two colour schemes

were offered in BR departmental 'Dutch' yellow and grey and EWS maroon, with three individually numbered models for each.

*See Table 3 for the full list of new wagons.*

## Outstanding year

Despite the awful impact of the COVID-19 pandemic, 2020 has been a marvellous year for new model releases with some truly outstanding models ranging from Hornby's sensational 'OO' gauge model of the diminutive Stephenson's *Rocket* 0-2-2 to Bachmann's exquisite and complex Ransomes and Rapier 45ton steam crane. The finesse and detailing that is achievable with today's manufacturing processes really is impressive – and it is not just the main manufacturers delivering this level of specification. Just look at Cavalex Models' new 'OO' gauge BBA wagon – the mesh decking is superb and the finely moulded cable runs beneath are very realistic. The detailing to the bogies really does raise the bar of what can be done, albeit at a price. Hattons Originals' new 'OO' gauge Class 66 is another stand-out model that not only looks the part but is available in more than 30 different identities off-the-shelf, while Dapol's 'OO' gauge LBSCR 'Terrier' 0-6-0T for Rails of Sheffield/Locomotion Models shows what can be achieved for a small locomotive with full detailing, provision for DCC/DCC sound and features such as firebox flicker.

Despite the background of the global pandemic and the inevitable disruption this has caused, it has been another impressive year for new model releases and there are plenty more to come – see *Forward to 2021* (pages 120-127) for more details. ∎

# GOING

In typical work stained condition, 'Dutch' liveried Class 31 31308 passes Little Bedwyn with 7Z31, a West Drayton-West Drayton crew training/ vacuum familiarisation working, on April 15 1999.
John Chalcraft/ Railphotoprints.uk.

# 'DUTCH'

Perhaps one of the most unloved and underrated parts of the late BR-era railway was that of the Departmental sector, whose dull grey colour scheme was vastly enhanced when the decision was taken to 'Go Dutch', as **EVAN GREEN-HUGHES** explains.

**E**VERY RAILWAY NEEDS ITS engineers - the people who lay the track, maintain the bridges, clean the ballast and look after the buildings. Without the engineers there would be no infrastructure on which the trains can run and it follows that without the engineers there would be no railway at all.

This fact seemed to be forgotten when in 1982 British Rail took the first tentative steps towards privatising its network. Prior to this, the organisation of the railways pretty much followed the pattern that it had in pre-nationalisation days which saw the system divided up into regional areas, each with its own layer of management. This all changed when freight traffic was separated off from passenger work, resulting in the introduction of a grey version of the 'large logo' blue livery and later the 'red stripe' version of the same scheme, which was applied specifically to goods engines.

In 1987 the system was further reorganised into a series of what were called 'business units', each charged with dealing with a specific type of traffic. On the passenger front this gave birth to Inter-City, Regional Railways, Network SouthEast and ScotRail while freight was divided up into Railfreight and Parcels. Almost immediately, further divisions took place within the freight sector with coal, metals, automotive, construction, petroleum, chemicals, minerals and international all getting their own managements, and with each receiving, at least nominally, its own locomotives, which were then marked up in suitable sector liveries.

These eye-catching liveries, which were all based on a three-tone grey scheme, were created with the assistance of the Roundel Design Group and were, compared with what had gone before, truly eye-catching.

Unfortunately, in reorganising the sectors, one important part of the railway was not given its own identity, and that was that which provided services to the engineers, with this being consigned to something which was rather condescendingly named, the 'general' sector. The purpose of this part of the railway seemed to be to deal with everything which didn't fall within anyone else's remit. Railfreight General was itself disbanded in 1989, with its freight duties moved to the distribution sector and its engineering function moved into a new organisation whose sole purpose was to support the Departmental sector. **»**

## Upheaval

The formation of the sectors caused a massive upheaval within British Rail: not only was management affected, but also the men on the ground found themselves working for an employer with a much narrower business remit than before. Previously locomotive crews could have found themselves working different kinds of traffic each day but now they would be exclusively dedicated to one kind of load or another and in the process to perhaps only one or two different types of traction, vastly reducing their flexibility and that of the network at times of unusual demand such as major engineering projects.

It's fair to say that not much of an attempt was made to brighten up the engines that the departmental sector was allocated. These were a rag-bag collection of mainly lower-powered types, many high on engine hours and which spent much of their lives parked up in depots awaiting the call to work at weekends and during holiday times when the engineers were busiest. Although 500 or so locomotives were repainted for the freight sector, new colours for the Departmentals were not very high on the list of priorities, with the result that most of them initially carried dirty and faded BR blue. Over time some did become due for Works attention and did receive bodywork upgrades, which included a repaint in a very dull shade of overall grey with yellow ends and black cab doors, which soon began to look dirty and which was possibly the worst colour scheme ever designed for a railway locomotive.

The next move took place in 1991 when the Departmental sector finally became fully independent and this resulted in a review of the rolling stock and locomotives it operated, and in particular of the colour scheme which had been adopted. Everyone agreed that the engineering department locomotives looked unduly poor in their existing scheme and as a result it was suggested that this could be considerably enhanced by the application of a large yellow band on the higher part of the

Just one Class 50 received departmental grey and yellow – 50015 *Valiant*. The English Electric Type 4 stands at Bristol St Philips Marsh depot on June 29 1991. Steve Carter/Railphotoprints.uk.

body side, which would run between the cabs. Whether this was by accident or design this scheme then bore a remarkable resemblance to that used by the Nederlandse Spoorwegen, or the Dutch Railways, with the result that it immediately became known as 'Dutch' livery.

## 'Dutch' diesels

The biggest number of locomotives to be painted in 'Dutch' livery were from the lower-powered classes, with the first Class 26 being painted at Eastfield in November 1990. Scotland eventually had 14 locomotives painted in this scheme with the bulk of them reliveried in 1990-1992. These included the 1958-built 26001-26005/26007, which were the earliest-built examples of these locomotives. The black cab doors and window surrounds were retained from the

former general livery, while depot plaques and numbers were fitted at opposite ends.

This attractive livery, with its half-height yellow front panel and cast depot plaques, particularly suited the Class 31 as the yellow side panels lined up with the upper bodyside grilles, and it readily identified those locomotives so painted as having a definite owner. This was particularly important at the time as departmental engines were often 'borrowed' without permission by depots which were short of motive power, usually to work Sprinter-substitute passenger trains, something which also led to the more drastic measure of disconnecting the electric train supply equipment in some of the locomotives preventing their use on passenger work and also leading to them being renumbered into the 31/5 series.

The first appearance of the 'Dutch' livery on a Class 33 took place in late 1990 with the yellow area being made slightly bigger so its bottom lined up with the cab and bodyside windows. The bulk of these locomotives had already received allover grey livery from 1989 onwards with some being repainted when transferred from the construction sector in 1992-1993. A total of 21 of the class received the 'Dutch' colours eventually with allocation being to parts of what had been the Southern Region. An unusual variant was that applied to 33051 which was given a white roof for railtour use, in which guise it travelled far off its usual working area.

On the Class 37s, the 'Dutch' livery was applied slightly differently in that the full yellow nose was retained, but the black was applied to the bonnet top and to the area around the windscreens. Again, the yellow stripe was organised in such a way as it lined up with the cantrail at the top and the cab windows at the bottom. This didn't work out quite as neatly as had the other classes in that the bottom of the yellow bisected several of the bodyside grilles. Although both the split headcode and the centre-headcode types were amongst those that received the colour scheme, locomotives allocated to departmental duties were those from the 37/0 sub-group, which basically consisted of engines that had never had

Class 33/0 33046 double heads with Class 33/1 33116 at Cole with an Eastleigh-Meldon empty ballast working on May 11 1993. 33116 carries the all over grey departmental scheme which predated the 'Dutch' version. John Chalcraft/Railphotoprint.uk

The grey and yellow departmental colour scheme was synonymous with the final years of the Class 33s on the Southern Region. On October 29 1998 33025, now shorn of its *Sultan* nameplates, approaches Wandsworth Road with 6068, the 12.56 Temple Mills-Hoo Junction engineers service. John Chalcraft/Railphotoprints.uk.

RAILWAY REALISM

class. These Class 73s were regarded as being on restricted duties, and would normally be stabled for the whole week, only appearing for limited mileages at the weekend.

## Grey and yellow wagons

The new 'Dutch' colours were also used on stock used by the departmental sector, which had previously been somewhat neglected, with many wagons carrying the plain black applied during the BR era. Other former main line stock had been used in their last-worn colours, in particular this had included a large number of 16ton steel open wagons displaced from coal and general duties, many of which had holes cut in their upper sides to prevent overloading with ballast or spoil, which was denser and therefore heavier than coal.

A large number of purpose-built ballast wagons were reliveried in this way, with these including all types used by the former 'Big Four' railways as well as similar wagons built during

upgrades or improvements. This also meant that many of the departmental engines were amongst the most run-down in the fleet and could often be seen working in extremely poor condition.

Although the Class 47 was regarded as one of the more useful classes and was considerably more powerful than the Type 2s and 3s, a total of 24 of the class received 'Dutch' livery. The livery suited this class well as the bodyside was less cluttered with grilles and the general pattern of lining up the base of the yellow stripe with the bottom of the cab windows was again applied. Where locomotives were named, the nameplates were fitted straddling the yellow panel and with the cast double arrows and depot plaques. A unique version of this livery was carried by 47308 which had its numbers just behind the cab doors on the yellow bodyside rather than on the cabside and as a result they were in black instead of white.

Only one Class 50 carried 'Dutch' livery when in BR ownership, working in the Plymouth area. This was 50015 *Valiant* which went on to be preserved at the East Lancashire Railway and the general paint layout mirrored that used on the Class 47, with the nameplates being fitted centrally and below the yellow area of the bodywork.

For the most demanding of its trains, a number of Class 56 heavy freight locomotives were retained by the Civil Engineers, with these receiving a version of the 'Dutch' scheme again very similar to that carried by the Class 47. Six locomotives were reliveried in this way, with these being allocated to Immingham and Toton but several years later these were taken back into normal freight stock, having Transrail stickers applied, though retaining their departmental liveries otherwise for a time.

Finally, on the Southern Region a number of electro-diesel Class 73s had been released by the parcels sector in around 1991 and along with some others these were transferred to departmental use. Twelve of these received 'Dutch' colours but there were a further four which remained in allover grey due to them being allocated to the Mechanical and Electrical Engineers department, rather than the Civil Engineers.

On this class, the yellow section took up around half of the bodyside, being of a much greater area than on other classes. This was so the bottom of the panel lined up with the cab windows, which are exceptionally deep on this

Right: **A number of the Class 26s received 'Dutch' colours in their final years. 26004 displays its final livery in the bay platform at Perth on August 16 1992.** John Chalcraft/Railphotoprints.co.uk.

Left: **As the railway moved into privatisation, the 'Dutch' colour scheme remained in the public eye, though often mixed with the new EWS colours and overlaid with operator's graphics. On March 15 1999 Class 37886 doubleheads with 37043 in Transrail branded 'Dutch' at the head of a mixed rake of engineering stock at Somerton.** John Chalcraft/Railphotoprints.uk.

Below: **Following privatisation a number of 'Dutch' liveried locomotives passed to Transrail and gained the freight operator's branding over their existing livery, and that saw their employment spread to other duties. Class 56 56036 passes East Usk Junction, Newport, with the 10.30 Grange Sidings-Llanwern coal working on August 27 1998 bearing Transrail branded 'Dutch' colours.** John Chalcraft/Railphotoprints.uk.

It wasn't just 'Dutch' locomotives which saw service on departmental trains. On July 15 1990 Class 50 50032 *Courageous* powers away from Twerton Tunnel working 'wrong line' with an engineering train made up of on-track plant and a rake of 'Dogfish' hoppers.
John Chalcraft/Railphotoprints.uk.

the BR era. These were repainted as they came through Works for refurbishment with the same colours being used as on the locomotives. Each wagon had a wide yellow stripe painted along the load area at the top of the wagon, but this did not run round the ends, which remained in plain grey. Lettering was stencilled on in white with each type of wagon also being identified by its unofficial nickname of 'Dogfish', 'Herring', 'Trout' or 'Catfish'. The bigger bogie 'Seacow' wagons also received the same treatment.

In the late 1980s a programme had been put under way to replace the old 'Grampus' ballast spoil wagons, with most of these being succeeded by the 'Rudd' which was created by using the chassis from 800 redundant 21-ton long-wheelbase coal hopper wagons. These were given heavily reinforced new bodies with three-section drop down sides. Again 'Dutch' livery was applied with the yellow stripe being at the top of the body, and this same general layout was also used for the 'Zander' which were constructed from former tank wagon chassis fitted with heavy duty box bodies and intended for the carriage of sand and similar materials. Interestingly, some of these were later to become owned by the Mainline sector, although they retained their 'Dutch' livery to which a Mainline sticker was added.

The 'Dutch' colours were not applied to the large bogie wagons used for the carriage of rails, as these were more usually painted in all-over yellow, though there were some exceptions

On a cold and frosty January 1 1992 Class 37/0 37207 stands at Yeovil Junction with a ballast train as part of Sunday engineering work. The wagons are vacuum brake 'Dogfish', three of which now carry the 'new' grey and yellow colour scheme.
John Chalcraft/
Railphotoprints.uk.

which were turned out in all-over grey. This was probably because it wasn't possible to get such a complicated livery on such a shallow bodyside.

## In private ownership

Between 1993 and 1997, the business of privatising the railways was finally completed, which again meant another change for the Departmental sector. The final move towards privatisation had taken so long because the concept had not been supported by the then Prime Minister, Margaret Thatcher, but it did go forward under her successor John Major and following the EU's 1991 directive which aimed to create a more competitive rail sector.

Under privatisation, responsibility for looking after the infrastructure fell to a new organisation, Railtrack, while much of the actual maintenance was taken over by a number of private companies. This inevitably led to changes within the departmental fleet, as no locomotives were taken over by Railtrack and instead the company was forced to hire them in from operators which themselves were renting them in from leasing companies. The same was true of rolling stock, which had also been parcelled out to the leasing companies as part of the deal.

It was the arrival of the large number of Class 66 locomotives into the freight sector that saw the gradual removal of the 'Dutch' livery from the national network. The private companies, who were by now largely in charge of engineering work, found it was more efficient to hire in modern traction, which would otherwise have been lying idle at the weekends, to work ballast and rail trains, rather than maintain a fleet of dedicated engines. Many of the locomotives that previously had been employed were soon withdrawn, although a few did pass to new owners for a few more years work in other sectors. The same was true of the wagon fleet,

'Dutch' locomotives could also be seen on some passenger services where extra motive power was required. Class 31s 31166 and 31146 stand at the new island platform at Welshpool with the 9.25am Birmingham-Pwllheli on August 15 1992. Brian Robbins/Railphotoprints.uk.

which had for many years comprised either redundant main line stock or repurposed vehicles but which was replaced with purpose-built and very efficient wagons such as self-loading high-capacity ballast carriers and the latest in on-track maintenance machines.

The end for the 'Dutch' livery did not come about all of a sudden, but instead it slipped into history gradually as locomotives and stock were withdrawn and replaced with new. For many years it remained in obscurity as modellers and enthusiasts alike were more attracted

to the new bright colours of the passenger and freight franchises but just recently there has been a resurgence in interest, leading even to the repainting of some preserved locomotives in this attractive colour scheme.

The 'Dutch' period was an interesting one for those who wish to follow Departmental trains. With its colourful paint scheme, array of historical and rebuilt wagons and elderly locomotives it presents considerable opportunities for the modeller, which perhaps are not available from other more well-known sectors of the railway. ∎

# *Building the* GREAT PART TWO CENTRAL RAILWAY

The first phase of our new project layout for the Yearbook is complete. **MIKE WILD** takes a closer look at how it will operate, its rolling stock and future plans for development.

**PHOTOGRAPHY, RICHARD WATSON**

**①** Robinson 'O4' 2-8-0 63601 rumbles through Quorn Magna station with a rake of 16ton mineral wagons as Thompson 'B1' 4-6-0 61138 arrives with a northbound passenger working.

A DEFINING part of the scene for our Great Central Railway layout is its rolling stock. We have completed the layout and now all the bullhead rail track has been weathered, while static grass has been built up around the railway and the goods yard sidings to blend everything together.

Detailing of a model railway can be an almost never-ending process and we've enjoyed putting the finishing touches (so far) to the overall scene – though we have plenty of plans to take what we have built further and enhance its appearance. The richly detailed static grass expanses have been enhanced with extra foliage, trees, bushes and Woodland Scenics new board fencing to give greater interest to draw the eye. As we said earlier in this Yearbook, the GCR was an open and neatly kept railway, although we needed some grass detailing around the trackbed to stop the scene from looking too clinical.

We've also introduced new elements including a water column between the main running lines – a common feature of GCR stations – using a Bachmann Scenecraft product while the platforms have been drilled to accept a set of matching green painted working gas lamps at four positions. Platform »

Above: **Quorn Magna signalbox has been scratchbuilt for the layout and features full interior detailing.**

benches have been borrowed from our Grosvenor Square detailing pack, but it is likely that we will make new ones for the layout in the future. Also added to the station beneath the canopy are Bachmann's new Scenecraft station vending machines and accessories which add a little touch of interest to that area.

Being the GCR, passengers are thin on the ground – in fact in all the photographs we've looked over to create this layout none of the BR era images we saw showed any passengers waiting for trains. One had a handful of crew and staff at Loughborough Central, but on reflection it is clear why this railway wasn't going to survive as part of the national network. Our platform has a single passenger checking his watch while we have a pair of station staff attending to platform trolleys and sack barrows.

The goods yard is a little busier with an arriving lorry load of casks, bags of coal waiting for onward movement and a collection of pallets, sleepers and redundant cable drums strewn

in the corner. The yard foreman's car is a red Volkswagen Beetle, and if you look really closely you can see he has had a reversing incident as it is missing its rear bumper. The even more eagle eyed will notice it has American specification 'towel rail' bumpers too – maybe that's just me?

The road over the main bridge is now complete following painting and weathering with Woodland Scenics paints with its population including a couple of cars and a Belle Vue coaches Duple Roadmaster on an excursion from Manchester.

## Operation

Down below the road, the railway is quiet, but in the distance the soft exhaust of a GCR Robinson 'O4' can be heard. Its shrill whistle carries through the still afternoon air and it then bursts under the road bridge in a cloud of steam heading a long rake of empty 16ton mineral wagons. It passes Thompson 'B1' 4-6-0 61138 heading a northbound passenger working and even though the 'O4' is travelling at »

### QUORN MAGNA LOCOMOTIVE FLEET

#### EASTERN REGION, 1950-1958

| LOCOMOTIVE | MANUFACTURER | DECODER/SOUND PROFILE |
|---|---|---|
| Robinson 'O4' 2-8-0 63601 | Bachmann | ESU LokSound/Howes |
| Robinson 'O4' 2-8-0 63598 | Bachmann | ESU LokSound/Howes |
| Robinson 'O4' 2-8-0 63762 | Bachmann | ZIMO/Digitrains |
| Robinson 'D11' 4-4-0 62667 | Bachmann | ZIMO/Digitrains |
| Gresley 'K3' 2-6-0 61869 | Bachmann | ZIMO/Digitrains |
| Gresley 'V2' 2-6-2 60862 | Bachmann | ESU LokSound/Howes |
| Gresley 'A3' 4-6-2 60043 | Hornby | ESU LokSound/Howes |
| Thompson 'O1' 2-8-0 63670 | Hornby | ESU LokSound/Howes |
| Thompson 'B1' 4-6-0 61138 | Hornby | ESU LokSound/Howes |
| Robinson 'J11' 0-6-0 64325 | Bachmann | ESU LokSound/Howes |
| Thompson 'O1' 2-8-0 63789 | Hornby | ESU LokSound/Howes |
| Thompson 'L1' 2-6-4T 67777 | Hornby | ZIMO/Digitrains |
| Riddles 'WD' 2-8-0 90448 | Bachmann | ESU LokSound/Howes |
| Riddles '9F' 2-10-0 92044 | Bachmann | ZIMO/Digitrains |

#### MIDLAND REGION, 1958-1966

| LOCOMOTIVE | MANUFACTURER | DECODER |
|---|---|---|
| Stanier '8F' 2-8-0 48706 | Hornby | ZIMO/Locoman Sounds |
| Stanier 'Black Five' 4-6-0 44694 | Hornby | D&H/Locoman Sounds |
| Stanier rebuilt 'Royal Scot' 4-6-0 46109 | Hornby | ESU LokSound/Howes |
| Riddles 'Britannia' 4-6-2 70007 | Hornby | D&H/Locoman Sounds |
| Riddles '5MT' 4-6-0 73049 | Bachmann | ZIMO/Digitrains |
| Riddles 'WD' 2-8-0 90015 | Bachmann | ZIMO/Digitrains |
| Riddles 'WD' 2-8-0 90254 | Bachmann | ESU LokSound/Howes |
| Riddles '9F' 2-10-0 92044 | Bachmann | ZIMO/Digitrains |
| Collett 'Hall' 4-6-0 5943 | Bachmann | ZIMO/Digitrains |
| Bulleid 'West Country' 4-6-2 34107 | Hornby | ZIMO/Digitrains |

**3** Gresley 'V2' 2-6-2 60860 *Durham School* passes non stop through Quorn Magna with the 'South Yorkshireman', though it appears the crew forgot to add the headboard today. In the goods yard Robinson 'J11' 64325 shunts its trio of sand tipplers and ex-GWR box van into the main siding before reforming its pick up goods for the next leg of its journey south.

**4** Stanier 'Black Fives' were regulars on the GCR following the change to Midland Region control. A pristine 44694 waits to depart with a rake of matching BR lined maroon Mk 1s.

📷5 The goods yard at Quorn Magna is still well used. The yard foreman's Beetle is parked outside the store building.

a fairly pedestrian 25mph with its loose coupled train, it soon disappears into the distance.

The locomotive had clearly seen better days. 63601 was built in the early 1910s and remarkably is still in service now, even though it is the mid 1950s – one day it will be preserved as part of the National Collection and return to its former GCR stamping ground. For now, the Eastern Region is still in control of the line which keeps these venerable locomotives in service.

Another shrill whistle comes as the Thompson 'B1' 4-6-0's driver readies for departure after hearing the guard blow his whistle. Its all BR lined maroon set of Mk 1s are destined for Nottingham.

The unmistakable clank of a 'WD' 2-8-0 is next to disturb the peace as 90448 clomps round the curve from the bridge with a mixed freight heading north behind the 'B1'. Its driver had the regulator closed on the approach, but now he can see the signals are clear, he opens up again and shatters the peace as the 'Austerity' picks up speed again.

It's become a busy day for northbound workings today as a little later a BR '9F' 2-10-0 moves comfortably through the station at the head of another rake of 16ton minerals which clank and rumble through the pointwork as the train takes the gentle curve ➤➤

📷6 It's now the late 1950s and the GCR is under Midland Region control. BR '9F' 2-10-0 92077 moves north with a coal train as rebuilt 'Royal Scot' 4-6-0 46109 *Royal Engineer* speeds south with parcels.

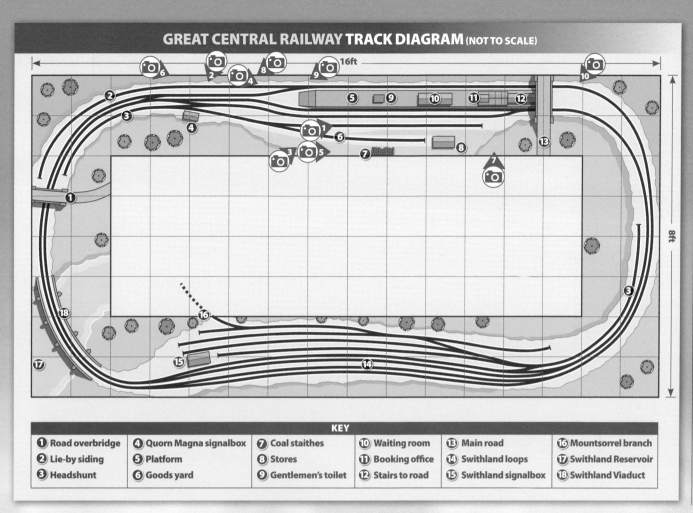

GREAT CENTRAL RAILWAY **TRACK DIAGRAM** (NOT TO SCALE)

16ft

8ft

| KEY | | | | | | | |
|---|---|---|---|---|---|---|---|
| **1** Road overbridge | **4** Quorn Magna signalbox | **7** Coal staithes | **10** Waiting room | **13** Main road | **16** Mountsorrel branch |
| **2** Lie-by siding | **5** Platform | **8** Stores | **11** Booking office | **14** Swithland loops | **17** Swithland Reservoir |
| **3** Headshunt | **6** Goods yard | **9** Gentlemen's toilet | **12** Stairs to road | **15** Swithland signalbox | **18** Swithland Viaduct |

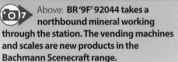 Above: **BR '9F' 92044 takes a northbound mineral working through the station. The vending machines and scales are new products in the Bachmann Scenecraft range.**

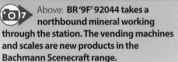 Below: **The driver of 'WD' 2-8-0 90448 opens the regulator again to accelerate the mixed goods after seeing the signals at Quorn Magna are clear.**

around the island platform and then disappears into the distance.

The signalbox bells ring again and levers are thrown back and forth to change points and signals to prepare for the arrival of 'J11' 0-6-0 64325 at the head of a short pick-up goods. It has just three sand tipplers and an ex-GWR 12ton box van in tow as it runs spiritedly into the goods loop on the east side of the station, rolling to a stop half way down the loop.

The guard climbs down and unhooks the wagons from the brake van and the 'J11' runs forward into the headshunt to take the 12ton van into the yard and collect new wagons for onward movement south to the junction station at Woodford Halse.

Meanwhile, another train is heading south and the signalbox has the signals off for a main line working to pass through the platform line while the 'J11' continues its business in the yard. This time it's the 'South Yorkshireman' in the hands of one of the last BR black 'V2' 2-6-2s. With whistle blowing, it steams under the road bridge non-stop.

## Midland interlopers

From 1958 the GCR passed into the control of the Midland Region for its final eight years of operation as a through route and with that change in management came new motive power. Now the previously Eastern Region dominated fleet has been joined by new BR Standards and ex-LMS designs such as the Stanier 'Black Five' 4-6-0, '8F' 2-8-0 and rebuilt 'Royal Scot' 4-6-0s.

We've skipped forward a few years to a new day in the GCR's life and in the lie-by siding Stanier '8F' 48706 is simmering at the head of a train formed of empty bogie bolster wagons and 16ton minerals. Its crew is managing the fire while they wait for the next northbound passenger train to overtake, a tricky balance between keeping the engine ready for departure and avoiding overheating the fire and causing the safety valves to lift.

Finally the train they are waiting for lumbers into view with a BR '5MT' 4-6-0 rounding the curve to the station with a rake of Maunsell SR green corridor stock on a through working from Poole to Bradford. As it passes the outer home signal, the driver of the '5MT' opens the regulator again and powers through the station to take the train closer to its destination.

Now the '8F' is free to move off and as soon as the signalman receives the line clear bell code, he pulls off the semaphore for the lie-by siding and releases the 2-8-0 which departs with a purposeful bark.

Parcels has remained an important commodity on the GCR and our next service is a southbound working in the hands of a rebuilt 'Royal Scot' 4-6-0. The engine is workstained but generally well kept, while its train is a collection of ex-LNER and BR era corridor stock with a couple of ventilated vans at the rear. In a brief surprise moment we see the 'Scot' crossing paths with another '9F' working a northbound coal train which passes straight through the station.

For now the railway has gone quiet again, but the keen eyed will be keeping watch for more »

trains at Quorn Magna. A Stanier 'Black Five' is likely on the next passenger service, but with Saturday approaching, there is a high possibility of interlopers from the Western and Southern making appearances, particularly if there is a football match or railtour planned. High on the hit list of possibilities are a GWR 'Modified Hall' 4-6-0 and one of Bulleid's air-smoothed 'West Country' 4-6-2s heading into 'foreign territory' on the GCR.

As you can see, the GCR had a diverse range of motive power over the years and you can sample more of its train formations in a dedicated feature on pages 106-111, for now though we are reaching the end of our visit to Quorn Magna, but don't worry, we will be back.

## The future

Completion of Quorn Magna is the first phase of this layout's construction, but we have much more to do to enhance what we have built so far for the Yearbook. For starters, we will be sanding down the platform surfaces to gain perfect joints and then repainting them too for a better appearance. Next in line is more detail for the platforms including wiring to power the station lamps, interior detail for the buildings and lighting. Then there are the signals – we are eagerly waiting on BR pattern upper quadrant bracket signals from Dapol for 'OO' to bolster the current range and once those are available, we will be replacing the temporary

fixed bracket which stands on the approach to the goods loop.

There will be other detailing elements to add too – and there is a plan to add point rodding to the layout, but the biggest project by far for the future is the other side of the layout, Swithland Sidings. This will be our winter challenge to bring that area up to standard to create a fully finished four-sided scenic layout which will be fit and ready to take up exhibition appearances in the future once the event timetable is back up and running. Fingers crossed, we might even be able to take Quorn Magna and Swithland Sidings to the Great Central Railway Model Event in the future to operate the layout alongside part of the

surviving real 'London Extension'.

Building this layout has been an entertaining and rewarding exercise and one which shows the potential of recent new arrivals on the scene – in particular Hattons new laser cut flat pack baseboard kits and Peco's bullhead track.

The biggest debate now is whether the layout should remain in the BR era or whether we should roll the clock forward to the present day in preservation? The jury is out on that decision, but maybe we should invest in a BR era set of buildings so we can ring the changes when we want to?

Look out for more on our Great Central Railway layout in future issues of *Hornby Magazine* during 2021. ■

A Stanier '8F' 2-8-0 is held in the lie-by siding to allow BR '5MT' 4-6-0 73030 to take priority with its Poole-Bradford working formed of Southern Region Maunsell corridor stock.

10 Left: **Stanier '8F' 48706** departs Quorn Magna after allowing the '5MT' to pass to take its string of empty bolster and mineral wagons north.

# Hornby's CEN

Hornby celebrated its 100th anniversary in 2020 with a spectacular line up of new products. Chief amongst those was its brand-new model of Stephenson's *Rocket* for 'OO' gauge reviving the former Tri-ang Railways 1963 product to 21st century standards. Two packs were produced – one for the centenary line up in Tri-ang Railways packaging (right) and a second (left) with different carriages and Railway Museum packaging for the main range.

2020 marked a very special occasion for Hornby as it welcomed its centenary year. **MARK CHIVERS** looks back at this milestone in the company's history and the products made to celebrate its 100th anniversary.

**W**HENEVER most people think of Hornby, they immediately think of model railways. Such is the power of the Hornby brand, which has been cultivated into the household name of today.

2020 has been a year of outstanding reflection for the manufacturer, as it marked 100 years since Frank Hornby first launched his 'O' gauge clockwork 0-4-0 locomotive, an extension of the Meccano system. At that moment a seed was planted that led to a company bearing his surname a century later producing highly detailed railway models with the finesse and running qualities that were but a pipe dream in those early pioneering days.

It is only natural that Hornby should want to celebrate this centenary year with a few special plans - but I doubt anyone expected the level and extent of these plans, with a raft of special Centenary models and collectables as well as a formidable release schedule of all-new tooling and re-liveries on existing models. Welcome to the Hornby 2020 range!

Pandemic aside, the year started with great promise as Hornby unveiled its proposed plans to celebrate this centenary year in style, with a collection of nostalgic limited-edition models spread across the following twelve months as well as special video promotions, a 'Golden Ticket' competition and more. First up, were four 'O' gauge replica models of the first Hornby Trains 0-4-0 locomotive and tender from 1920, offered in four different colour schemes as 2710 to cover London & North Western Railway black, Midland Railway maroon, Caledonian Railway blue and Great Northern green. Each of these tinplate collector's items was to reflect Frank Hornby's original design, although rather than a clockwork mechanism they would be up to modern standards with 12volt DC motors, three-rail pick-up, etched metal numberplates and each limited to just 100 models, presented in packaging reminiscent of the period.

And so the scene was set for the rest of this inspirational and exciting range. It was clear that the planned models were not just a random selection, but a carefully and meticulously considered series of 'OO' gauge products that were interleaved with Hornby's history through the years from the eye-catching blue boxed Hornby

# TENARY

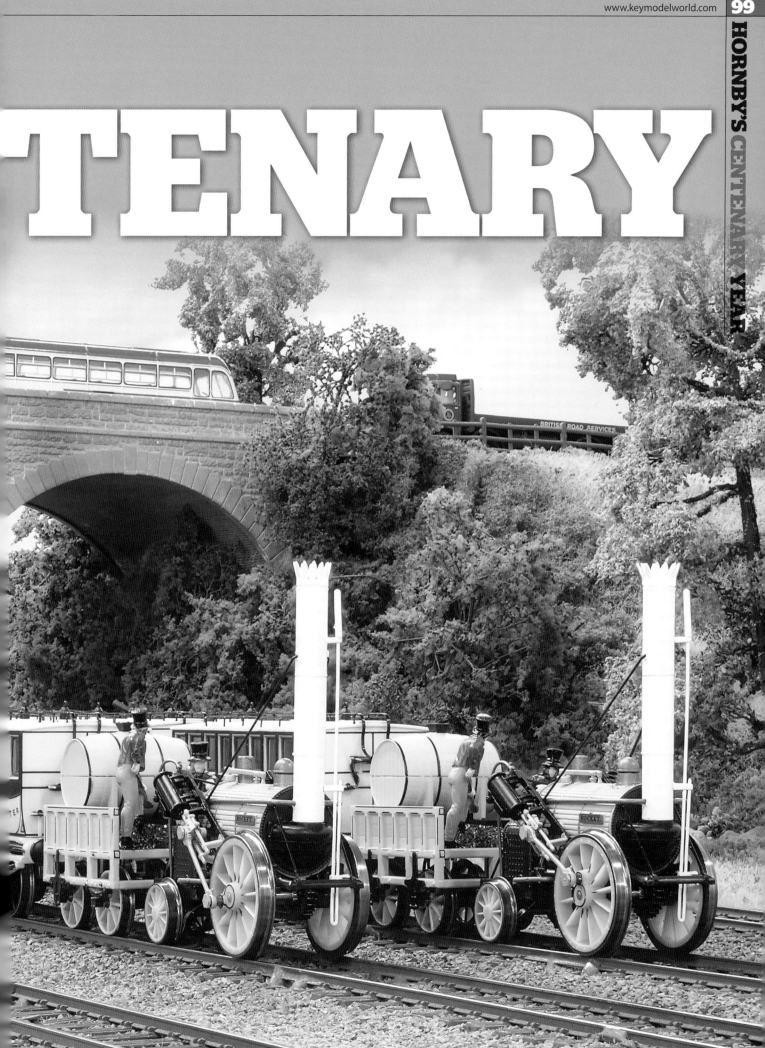

Dublo train set replicating the first 1938 train set, this time with the latest Gresley 'A4' 4-6-2 tooling and detailed Gresley 61ft 6in corridor coaches, to the model credited with turning Hornby's fortunes around in 2000 – Bulleid rebuilt 'Merchant Navy' 4-6-2 35028 *Clan Line*, now with gold-plated exterior metal parts. It is hard to believe that this model is now 20 years old; how time has flown since it was unveiled alongside the full-size engine at a special ceremony at Stewart's Lane depot in London all those years ago.

Given Hornby Dublo played a large part in the company's history, it was no surprise that further models would be included, but who would have guessed a bespoke diecast metal body would be tooled for Hornby's high-fidelity 'OO' gauge model of LMS 'Duchess' 4-6-2 6231 *Duchess of Atholl* in LMS maroon, reflecting the Hornby Dublo model from the 1940s? This superbly finished model looked the part, ran superbly and proved a popular seller, no doubt due to the extremely limited number produced – just 500 in total.

Mind you, not every decision taken was as straightforward as we would like to think, partially due to ownership changes through the years. For example, previous brand names associated with the Hornby name such as Dinky and Tri-ang were no longer owned by the manufacturer. As a result, some intentions were revised, such as the Dublo Diecast vehicle line up based on the Oxford Diecast 1:76 scale range, which pays homage to the Dinky Diecast models launched in the late 1950s, supplied in bespoke cardboard boxes with tissue-wrapped models. Vehicles issued included a MG TC, Morris J van, VW T2 van, Scammell mechanical horse and trailer, Fordson tractor and an Austin K8 van with an attractive Margate Hotel and Boarding Association finish, further cementing the company's roots on the South Coast from the mid-1950s. And, while on the subject of vehicles, Hornby announced

a further colourful commission for the Centenary range during the Summer with two versions of Corgi's 1:76 scale Bristol Lodekka bus in Hornby inspired livery. It will appear in Hornby red with a selection of past company logos applied and two route options – 20 Binns Road, reflecting the establishment of the model railway business in 1920 and 64 Westwood, recalling the year that Lines Brothers acquired the company.

## Special editions

Not all plans needed to be revised and Hornby's ambitious intention to retool one of Tri-ang's outstanding and possibly smallest 'OO' gauge locomotives from 1963, Stephenson's *Rocket* 0-2-2, came to fruition and they were able to acquire use of the original Tri-ang Railways branding to create a stunning limited edition package containing the all-new locomotive and three highly-detailed coaches (*Times, Despatch, Experience*) in Liverpool and Manchester Railway colours. For the first time, the model would be a true scale model too. It also

Hornby's 100 year history has so many highlights, including its long association with the Gresley 'A4' 4-6-2 which started in 1938 when the first Hornby Dublo version was released. Here its present day model of the 'A4' as 4468 *Mallard* poses between its NHS Thank You limited edition Class 800 and the limited edition centenary edition of Stephenson's *Rocket* illustrating the breadth of its product range perfectly.

The ever popular Peckett 'W4' 0-4-0ST was announced in works grey as part of the 2020 centenary collection.

**Left:** To support the NHS Hornby announced a limited edition of GBRf Class 66 66731 *Capt. Tom Moore A True British Inspiration* immediately after it was named at the end of April 2020. Such was its popularity that the production run was increased from 500 to 3,500 units. Sales of the 'OO' Class 66 raised £140,000 for the NHS.

**Right:** *Smokey Joe* is the longest standing model in the Hornby catalogue having been introduced in 1981 and never removed since. For the 2020 centenary it regained its metal handrails and full livery as a commemorative model.

The 2020 model of 6231
*Duchess of Atholl* is set to become
a sought-after collector's edition.
Just 500 were made with a die-cast
body recreating the original version
of the Stanier 'Duchess' launched by
Hornby Dublo in 1947. Here 6231 threads
through Topley Dale station with a rake of
Stanier Period III carriages in tow.

Hornby celebrated its 100th anniversary with an impressive array of special editions plus a couple of surprises too. This is a small selection of its 2020 limited editions.

featured a 6-pin Digital Command Control (DCC) decoder socket and lots of etched metal parts.

Just 1,500 packs were to be produced in commemorative Tri-ang Railways branded packaging, while a further run would be produced for the main range in Railway Museum branded packaging for those not wishing to pay a premium for the special limited edition. Later in the year, Hornby unveiled further plans for the *Rocket*, announcing a newly tooled Open Third vehicle to further enhance its appeal during its Hornby 100 Social Media takeover in the summer.

It is perhaps easy to forget how much of Hornby's history is influenced by Tri-ang, part of the Lines Brothers toy empire, and before that Rovex Plastics. So, further limited editions were planned around these with a replica Rovex train set, emulating the original 1950s packaging and containing Hornby's latest LMS 'Princess Royal' 4-6-2 in BR lined black and a pair of Stanier corridor coaches. The striking cover artwork features the 'Princess Royal' breaking through, just like the original. Meanwhile, when considering the Tri-ang Hornby period, the team decided upon last-built steam locomotive BR '9F' 2-10-0 92220 *Evening Star* in BR lined green with late crests. This seemed rather apt as when this newly-tooled model was released in 1972 it also marked the end of the Tri-ang Hornby era, as the company was about to become Hornby Railways, having just been acquired by new owners, Dunbee Combex Marx. Incidentally, the full-size locomotive had also been built in 1960 - another anniversary to commemorate.

When considering a limited-edition model from the 1980s, the

team shied away from glamorous tooling and decided upon the compact Class '0F' 0-4-0ST 56025 *Smokey Joe*. This particular locomotive has been in the Hornby range for many years and was produced to a price point in the 1980s, as the development team at the time were tasked to bring the

**Above: Hornby's 2020 catalogue artwork is one to remember with the iconic APT crossing over Stephenson's *Rocket* – the grandfather of the modern steam locomotive.**

costs within a certain budget. This resulted in some of the metal parts being removed and decoration simplified for its use as a solo item and in train sets during this period. However, for its Centenary range appearance *Smokey Joe* has been reunited with its metal handrails and features fully lined decoration with embellishments, plus it is presented in the Hornby Railways ribbon-style packaging from the period too.

Given the investment in newly tooled models that we have come to expect in recent times, it is a sobering thought that this has not always been the case. For a period in the 1980s and 1990s, the Hornby brand relied heavily on its back catalogue when it came to new releases. However, in the late 1990s Hornby acquired tooling from another manufacturer that enabled it to inject some much-needed detail into the 'OO' gauge range. One of those was the London Brighton & South Coast

Railway (LBSCR) 'Terrier' 0-6-0T, a model which went on to spawn many identities in the Hornby range until a new and improved example was introduced in 2019.

To celebrate this locomotive's role within the company's history, the team added 'Terrier' 45 *Merton* to the Centenary collection in Stroudley improved engine green, which not only cements its place as one of the models that helped plug the gap ahead of further investment in new tooling into the 2000s, but the name also links nicely to the former Tri-ang Works in South West London. As with other models in this fascinating collection, the model appears in retro-style packaging, in this case the distinctive 1990s style Top Link red artwork. Just 1,000 were manufactured.

As the new millennium approached, so too did a new chapter in Hornby's history as tooling and manufacture were transferred to the far east. One of

**The artwork for Hornby's Rovex trainset recaptures the original design with black liveried Stanier 'Princess' 46201 bursting through the box front.**

the models under development at this time was the Bulleid rebuilt 'Merchant Navy' 4-6-2, which was like no other locomotive that had gone before in the range, certainly in terms of detailing and running characteristics. Its slow speed running, weighty demeanour and stunning looks ensured healthy sales, so much so that it is considered the locomotive that improved fortunes for the manufacturer and set it on the path it is on today. To celebrate this fact, the model was to receive the gold-plated treatment for its Centenary appearance together with a wooden plinth, 18ct gold-plated track and packaging style from the 2000s.

Finally, it may be a small model but Hornby's 'OO' Peckett 'W4' 0-4-0ST has had a big impact with modellers since its launch in October 2015. For its Centenary outing this delightful locomotive was finished as Peckett 614 in Peckett and Sons photographic grey and a cast resin builder's plate was included in the box too, rounding off the sensational Hornby 100 collection. Given the popularity of this humble 0-4-0ST, 2,000 models were planned.

And there you have it - what a collection it has turned out to be! An

The 1920s three-rail 'O' gauge tinplate era was commemorated with a series of four limited edition replicas of the original Hornby No. 1 locomotive. This is the LNWR black version as 2710.

impressive array of limited-edition collectables that commemorate key stages in the evolution of Hornby's rich heritage together with appropriate packaging for each period, such as the inclusion of the young lad on the Hornby Dublo train set, recreating the 1950s style Dublo Diecast boxes and the striking image on the Rovex train set. Not only that, just to add another exciting layer to proceedings, Hornby unveiled plans for a 'Golden Ticket' promotion with ten special tickets included within boxes across selected Centenary

range items. Nine of these tickets were for a cash amount to be spent on the Hornby website, while the tenth ticket would entitle the holder and a guest to a very special trip on the Belmond British Pullman train.

However, this was only part of the celebratory year's story, as Hornby also included an ambitious plan of newly tooled models too, no doubt encouraged by its plans for the centenary. What better way to celebrate the first 100 years of Hornby's association with model railways than to add seven newly-tooled 'OO' gauge projects

to the roster too, including the LNER's experimental 'W1' 4-6-4, Thompson 'A2/2' and 'A2/3' 4-6-2s, BR '2MT' 2-6-0 and BR Class 91 Bo-Bo electric. In normal times, just these models would be sufficient, but given the year's significance an all-new model of BR's Class 370 Advanced Passenger Train was also unveiled, with sufficient vehicles to run up to a full 14-car prototypical set. If this was not enough, new BR Mk 1 Restaurant Buffet cars were also added, as was a full nine-car rake of LMS 'Coronation Scot' carriages in LMS Caledonian

An undoubted highlight of the main 2020 range is the creation of Gresley's unique 'W1' 4-6-4 for 'OO' gauge in both original and rebuilt forms. The final decoration samples arrived in October for inspection ahead of the models' expected release in early 2021. Here the three original 'Hush Hush' versions are joined by the rebuilt example in LNER Garter blue at Topley Dale.

To reflect the late 1930s period, a Hornby Dublo train set featuring 4498 *Sir Nigel Gresley* and two Gresley teak coaches was issued, recreating the manufacturers first 'OO' gauge train set from 1938.

blue. (See *Forward to 2021* for more details on pages 120-127).

## Supporting the NHS

Of course, little did anyone know at the time of the range launch that a pandemic would create the degree of disruption to our daily lives and work routines. With a lockdown in place and staff within an overstretched NHS working tirelessly to cope with the upsurge in admissions to hospital, despite well documented issues with the supply of Personal Protection Equipment, one name came to the fore in April – Captain Sir Tom Moore. 'Captain Tom' as he was dubbed by the media, was approaching his 100th birthday and planned to do 100 laps of his garden to raise funds for NHS Charities Together. His aim was to raise £1,000, but with the media attention, this target was subsequently raised and eclipsed, with over £32million eventually being raised by the day of his 100th birthday.

To commemorate this amazing achievement, GB Railfreight named one of its Class 66 Co-Co diesels 66731 *Capt. Tom Moore – A True British Inspiration* on April 30. Hornby quickly followed suit and announced that it would be producing a limited-edition 'OO' gauge model of 66731, with all proceeds from the model's sales through the Hornby website being donated to NHS Charities Together. The initial plan was to produce 500 models, but demand for the newly announced model immediately outstretched that volume such that 3,500 models were eventually produced and £140,000 was raised for the charity. Hornby pulled out all the stops and the model arrived with customers during the Summer.

Buoyed by this, Hornby also launched its NHS livery competition in May. Participants were encouraged to create a striking livery to adorn a Class 800 IET power car, while also raising further funds for the NHS charities. The winning entry was applied to two 'OO' gauge power cars with one being presented to the winner – James Lodge – while the other was raffled through a Just Giving page.

In total, a further £4,494 was raised. Incidentally, the power cars also received an official 'R' number and featured bespoke packaging and a *very* limited-edition certificate – in fact the NHS Thank You Class 800 power car may just be Hornby's most limited-edition official item ever.

So, there you have it – a very special year for Hornby in so many ways. Congratulations on the first 100 years of innovative, exciting and fun model railway releases - here's to the next 100! ∎

# GREAT CENTRAL

## MAIN LINE

Despite its lamented closure in the late 1960s, sections of the Great Central 'London Extension' still see regular train services today, thanks to the efforts of preservationists.

**MARK CHIVERS** presents a selection of passenger and freight formations from two distinctly different periods in the line's history.

The Great Central Railway saw a variety of ex-LNER and ex-LMS motive power at the head of its trains during the British Railways era with the change to Midland Region control from 1958. In the final week of GCR services south of Rugby, Stanier 'Black Five' 4-6-0 45222 takes water at Rugby Central with the 5.15pm Nottingham Victoria-Marylebone in 1966. Patrick Russell/Rail Archive Stephenson.

**W**HILST THE GREAT CENTRAL (GC) 'London Extension' never quite fulfilled its potential, it still witnessed a good deal of traffic along the route through the years with passenger services to and from London, inter-regional trains, railtours and special charters, plus a spectrum of freight services ranging from humble pick-up goods to lengthy (and heavy) coal trains bound for the capital.

From a modelling perspective, the GC main line presents some exciting opportunities as a diverse assortment of motive power and rolling stock appeared on the line. Handily, some of the line's main passenger train formations between the East Midlands and London ran to perhaps four or five vehicles, which enables prototypical length trains to be represented in less space - ideal if this is a limiting factor. Allied to this, the line had come under the auspices of BR's Eastern Region following nationalisation with appropriate rolling stock and traction until a change of control in 1958 resulted in the migration to more Midland inspired motive power.

As a result, it is possible to model the route with a diverse collection of 'OO' gauge locomotives to suit the period. Bachmann's prolific range includes 'J11' 0-6-0s, 'D11'/'D11/1' 4-4-0s, 'B1' 4-6-0s, 'V2' 2-6-2s, 'O4' 2-8-0s, 'WD' 2-8-0s, 'Fairburn' 2-6-4Ts, 'Jubilee' 4-6-0s, BR Standard '5MT' 4-6-0s, '9F' 2-10-0s and more, while Hornby's collection of 'B1' 4-6-0s, 'Royal Scot' and 'Patriot' 4-6-0s, 'Black Five' 4-6-0s, 'O1' 2-8-0s, '8F' 2-8-0s, BR 'Britannia' 4-6-2s and BR '9F' 2-10-0s expand the potential roster further. In addition, since the GC main line also hosted inter-regional traffic, railtours and special trains, further

interesting motive power also appeared, such as GWR 'Hall' 4-6-0s, LMS 'Princess Coronation' 4-6-2s, SR 'West Country' 4-6-2s, the occasional BR Class 47 Co-Co diesel and many more.

But that is only part of the story, as you can also model the Great Central Railway (GCR) between Loughborough Central and Leicester North in its present-day preservation era guise which presents further opportunities with a wealth of modelling potential. Just some of the 'OO' gauge locomotives you could utilise include Bachmann's Fowler 'Jinty' 0-6-0T, Ivatt '2MT' 2-6-0, BR '4MT' 2-6-0, GWR 'Modified Hall' 4-6-0, BR '5MT' 4-6-0, Robinson 'O4' 2-8-0, BR '9F' 2-10-0, plus BR Class 08, 20, 25, 37, 45, 47, 55 diesels and Class 101 DMU. Meanwhile, the Hornby 'OO' gauge range includes the GWR 'Hall' and 'King' 4-6-0s, SR 'Schools' 4-4-0, SR 'King Arthur' 4-6-0, SR air-smoothed 'Battle of Britain' 4-6-0, SR rebuilt 'Battle of Britain/West Country' 4-6-0s, LMS 'Black Five' 4-6-0, BR 'Britannia' 4-6-2, LMS '8F' 2-8-0, together with BR Class 08, 31 and 50 diesels. New manufacturer EFE Rail's range includes 'OO' gauge 'J94' 0-6-0STs, while Heljan's 'OO' gauge range features BR Class 26, 27 and 33 Bo-Bo diesels, with new model projects currently underway for Class 25, 45 and 47 locomotives. Hornby is also developing a new 'OO' gauge model of the BR Standard '2MT' 2-6-0, two of which are currently located at the GCR.

Of course, such a diverse collection of locomotives requires a good selection of carriages and wagons to add further variety. Between them, the main manufacturers produce an extensive range for 'OO' gauge spanning many decades including Bachmann's LNER Thompson stock, LMS 'Porthole' coaches and BR Mk 1 vehicles, together with Hornby's LNER Gresley and Thompson non-corridor suburban coaches,

Gresley 61ft 6in corridor stock, LMS Stanier 57ft non-corridor and corridor stock, plus a growing range of BR Mk 1s which is also due to be expanded with a Restaurant Buffet (RB) car later this year. Further variety can be sprinkled into the equation with other regional stock including GWR 60ft Collett carriages (Bachmann), SR Bulleid 63ft coaches (Bachmann), SR Bulleid 59ft vehicles (Hornby) and Maunsell coaches (Hornby).

Freight stock is equally well represented in 'OO' with an outstanding selection of wooden and steel-bodied open wagons and 12ton ventilated/non-ventilated vans covering Eastern, Midland and BR examples, along with hopper wagons, bogie bolsters, specialist vehicles and brake vans from Accurascale, Bachmann, Hornby and Oxford Rail (see tables).

The following selection of formations represents a taster of services on the 'London Extension' in the late 1950s/1960s, with the later preservation-era examples reflecting services running on the Loughborough Central to Leicester North stretch. These later train formations also have a more 'anything-goes' appearance in terms of traction and rolling stock, which is accurate for the period. In addition, the preservation-era formations also include some of the demonstration freight and Travelling Post Office (TPO) services operated at selected times on the line in recent years, making use of its large collection of 16ton steel mineral open wagons ('Windcutters'), 12ton box vans and TPO carriages, all of which go together to create some interesting and colourful formations. To keep the formations manageable, we have selected examples which dont' exceed 10 coaches. Where a particular 'OO' gauge model is currently unavailable, an alternative vehicle may have been substituted. ∎

**TRAIN FORMATIONS**

## BR ERA PASSENGER FORMATIONS

LNER 'B1' 4-6-0, BR lined black with early crests (Bachmann/Hornby), BR Mk 1 BSK*, CK, FK, Gresley 61ft 6in RF, Mk 1 TSO, SK, BSK, Gresley 61ft 6in SK, SK – BR maroon, except *BR carmine and cream. ● **Date:** 1957 ● **Service:** Marylebone to Manchester ● **Location:** Marylebone

LNER 'V2' 2-6-2, BR lined green with late crests (Bachmann), Gresley 61ft 6in BCK, BR Mk 1 CK, CK, SK, SK, BSK, Gresley 61ft 6in SK*, RF, BR Mk 1 CK, BSK – BR maroon, except *BR carmine and cream. ● **Date:** 1959 ● **Service:** 'The South Yorkshireman' ● **Location:** Aylesbury

LNER 'D11/1' 4-4-0, BR lined black with early crests (Bachmann), Gresley 61ft 6in BCK, BR Mk 1 SK, Gresley 61ft 6in SK, BCK – BR maroon
● **Date:** 1959 ● **Service:** Nottingham Vic. to Marylebone. ● **Location:** Quorn

BR '5MT' 4-6-0, BR lined green with late crests (Bachmann), Maunsell BSK, SK, SK, CK, CK, SK, SK, BSK – BR green
● **Date:** 1963 ● **Service:** Portsmouth Harbour to Nottingham Vic. ● **Location:** Loughborough

BR 'Britannia' 4-6-2, BR lined green, late crests (Hornby), BR Mk 1 BSK, SK, SK, CK, SK, BSK, Stanier SK, BSK – BR maroon
● **Date:** 1963 ● **Service:** Nottingham Victoria to Marylebone. ● **Location:** East Leake

GWR 'Hall' 4-6-0, BR lined green with late crests (Bachmann/Hornby), Stanier BSK, SK, FK, BSK, SK, CK, SK, BSK
● **Date:** 1964 ● **Service:** Poole to Bradford ● **Location:** Loughborough Central

LMS 'Royal Sot' 4-6-0, BR lined green with late crests (Hornby), BR Mk 1 BSK, SK, CK, BSK, Stanier non-corridor C, BS – BR maroon
● **Date:** 1964 ● **Service:** Empty Coaching Stock to Nottingham Victoria ● **Location:** New Basford

LMS 'Black Five' 4-6-0, BR lined black with late crests (Hornby), Stanier BSK, BR Mk 1 SK, CK, BSK – BR maroon
● **Date:** 1965 ● **Service:** Marylebone to Nottingham Victoria. ● **Location:** Brackley Central

BR Brush Type 4 Co-Co, BR two-tone green (Bachmann/Heljan/ViTrains), BR Mk 1 BSK, Stanier SK, SK, SK, BR Mk 1 RB, Stanier SK, SK, SK, SK, BSK – BR maroon
● **Date:** 1965 ● **Service:** Football special (to Wembley) ● **Location:** Calvert

SR rebuilt 'Merchant Navy' 4-6-2, BR lined green with late crests (Hornby), BR Mk 1 BSK, SO, SO, SO, RB, SO, SO, SO, SO, BSK – BR green
● **Date:** 1966 ● **Service:** LCGB 'The Great Central Rail Tour'. ● **Location:** Quorn

## BR ERA FREIGHT FORMATIONS

LNER 'J11' 0-6-0, BR black with early crests (Bachmann), two 16ton steel mineral wagons, Conflat with container*, 12ton vent van*, BR 20ton brake van* - BR grey, except *BR bauxite. ● **Date:** 1959 ● **Service:** Pick-up goods ● **Location:** Dinting

LNER 'O4' 2-8-0, BR black with early crests (Bachmann), seven-plank open wagon, five-plank open wagon, SR 12ton vent van*, 21ton steel mineral open wagon, two nine-plank mineral open wagons, four 21ton steel mineral open wagons, five-plank open wagon, five-plank open wagon, seven-plank open wagon, BR 20ton brake van* – BR grey, except *BR bauxite. ● **Date:** 1954 ● **Service:** Mixed freight ● **Location:** Ollerton

BR Standard '9F' 2-10-0, BR black with late crests (Bachmann/Hornby), four 16ton steel mineral open wagons, two seven-plank open wagons, 13ton high-sided 16ton steel mineral open wagon, seven-plank open wagon, eight 16ton steel mineral open wagons, two SR 12ton vent vans*, two 16ton steel mineral open 16ton steel mineral open wagons, five-plank open wagon, 12ton vent van*, three five-plank open wagons, BR 20ton brake van – BR grey, except *BR bauxite.

LNER 'O4' 2-8-0, BR black with late crests (Bachmann), 14 27ton iron ore wagons, BR 20ton brake van* - BR grey, except *BR bauxite.
● **Date:** 1962 ● **Service:** Iron ore ● **Location:** Bulwell North Junction

LNER 'O1' 2-8-0, BR black with late crests (Bachmann), 20 16ton steel mineral open wagons, BR 20ton brake van* – BR grey, except *BR bauxite.
● **Date:** 1963 ● **Service:** Coal empties ● **Location:** Tibshelf Town

| SUITABLE 'OO' GAUGE PASSENGER AND PARCELS STOCK | | |
|---|---|---|
| **TYPE** | **LIVERY** | **MANUFACTURER** |
| BR Mk 1 BG/BSK/CK/FK/FO/RB/RU/RFO/RMB/SK/TSO | BR crimson and cream/maroon/green | Bachmann |
| BR Mk 1 GUV/CCT | BR blue/maroon | Bachmann |
| BR Mk 1 BG/BSK/BSO/CK/FO/RB^/SK/SO/TSO | BR crimson and cream/maroon/green | Hornby |
| BR Mk 1 RB/RB(R) | BR maroon/green | Mainline/Replica Railways |
| GWR 60ft Collett BCK/BSK/CK/FK/TK | BR chocolate and cream/crimson and cream/maroon | Bachmann |
| SR Bulleid 63ft semi-open BSK/CK/SK/SO | BR carmine and cream/green | Bachmann |
| SR Bulleid 59ft BSK/CK | BR green | Hornby |
| SR Maunsell BCK/BSK/CK/FK/SK/SO/RB | BR green | Hornby |
| LMS 57ft PI BTK/CK/TK | BR maroon | Bachmann |
| LMS 57ft Stanier non-corridor BT, C, T | BR maroon | Hornby |
| LMS 12-wheel dining car | BR crimson and cream/maroon | Dapol/Hornby |
| LMS 'Porthole' BFK/BTK/CK/FK/FO/TK | BR crimson and cream/maroon | Bachmann |
| LMS Stanier PIII 50ft BG | BR maroon | Bachmann/Hornby |
| LMS Stanier PIII BSK/FK/SK | BR crimson and cream/maroon | Hornby |
| LMS Stanier PIII BSK/CK | BR crimson and cream/maroon | Dapol |
| LMS Stanier 'Stove R' | BR crimson/maroon | Key Publishing/Dapol |
| LNER 51ft Gresley/Thompson non-corridor BT, C, F, T | BR crimson/maroon | Hornby |
| LNER 59ft/63ft Thompson BG/BCK/BTK/CK/FK/TK | LNER teak/BR crimson and cream | Bachmann |
| LNER 61ft 6in Gresley BCK/BG/FK/TK/Buffet | LNER teak/BR crimson and cream/maroon | Hornby |
| **Notes:** ^ forthcoming model | | |

open wagon*, 16ton slope sided steel open wagon, wagons, 16ton slope sided steel open wagon, two
**Date:** 1959 ● **Service:** Mixed freight ● **Location:** Charwelton

| VEHICLE DESIGNATIONS | |
|---|---|
| **BG** | Gangwayed Brake |
| **BCK** | Corridor Brake Composite |
| **BCL** | Brake Composite Lavatory |
| **BPOT** | Post Office Brake Tender |
| **BS** | Brake Second |
| **BSK** | Corridor Brake Second |
| **BT** | Brake Third |
| **BTL** | Brake Third with Lavatory |
| **BTK** | Corridor Brake Third |
| **C** | Composite |
| **CL** | Composite Lavatory |
| **CCT** | Covered Carriage Truck |
| **CK** | Corridor Composite |
| **FK** | Corridor First |
| **FO** | Open First |
| **GUV** | General Utility Van |
| **PMV** | Parcels and Miscellaneous Van |
| **POS** | Post Office Sorting |
| **POT** | Post Office Tender (stowage) |
| **RB** | Restaurant Buffet |
| **RB(R)** | Restaurant Buffet (Refurbished) |
| **RC** | Restaurant Car |
| **RK** | Kitchen Car |
| **RFO** | Restaurant First Open |
| **RMB** | Restaurant Miniature Buffet |
| **RU** | Restaurant Car Unclassed |
| **RUO** | Restaurant Unclassed Open |
| **S** | Second |
| **SK** | Corridor Second |
| **SO** | Open Second |
| **TK** | Corridor Third |
| **TO** | Open Third |
| **TSO** | Tourist Open Second |

## BR ERA FREIGHT FORMATIONS

Stanier '8F' 2-8-0, BR black with late crests (Hornby), 20+ 16ton steel mineral open wagons, BR 20ton brake van – BR grey.
● **Date:** 1963 ● **Service:** Coal ● **Location:** Woodford Halse

BR '9F' 2-10-0, BR black with late crests (Bachmann/Hornby), 25+ 16ton steel mineral open wagons, BR 20ton brake van* - BR grey, except *BR bauxite.
● **Date:** 1963 ● **Service:** Coal ● **Location:** Rugby Central

'WD' 2-8-0, BR black with late crests (Bachmann), 16ton steel mineral open wagon, four one-plank 'Lowfit' wagons, five 21ton hoppers, 12ton vent van*, BR 20ton brake van* - BR grey, except *BR bauxite. ● **Date:** 1963 ● **Service:** Mixed freight ● **Location:** Rugby Central

LMS '8F' 2-8-0, BR black with late crests (Hornby), 12ton pipe wagon*, two 12ton vent vans*, two bogie bolster Cs, 12ton tank wagon**, 16ton steel mineral open wagon, three bogie bolster Cs, 15 16ton steel mineral open wagons, two SR 12ton vent vans*, 10 16ton steel mineral open wagons, BR 20ton brake van* - BR grey, except *BR bauxite and ** black.

LMS 'Royal Scot' 4-6-0, BR lined green with late crests (Hornby), Stanier BG, BR Mk 1 BG, BG, BG, BG, Stanier BSK, BR Mk 1 BG, BG, BG, BG, Stanier BG, three 12ton vent vans* - BR maroon, except *BR bauxite. ● **Date:** 1964 ● **Service:** Nottingham to Marylebone Parcels ● **Location:** Charwelton

## PRESERVATION

LNER 'D11' 4-4-0, GCR lined green (Bachmann), BR Mk 1 BCK, TSO, SO, RB, TSO, TSO*, TSO* - BR carmine and cream, except *BR blue and grey.
● **Date:** 1990 ● **Service:** Loughborough Central to Leicester North ● **Location:** Loughborough

BR 'Britannia' 4-6-2, BR lined green with late crests (Hornby), BR Mk 1 BG*, TSO, TSO, BCK, SK, SK, FK, RFO** - BR chocolate and cream, except *BR maroon and **BR carmine and cream. ● **Date:** 2018 ● **Service:** Loughborough Central to Leicester North ● **Location:** Quorn

LMS '3F' 0-6-0T, BR black with early crests (Bachmann), BR Mk 1 FK, SK, BCK, SK – BR chocolate and cream.
● **Date:** 2019 ● **Service:** Loughborough to Rothley ● **Location:** Quorn

SR air-smoothed 'West Country' 4-6-2, BR lined green with early crests (Hornby), BR Mk 1 TSO, TSO, Gresley 61ft 6in Buffet*, BR Mk 1 TSO, BSK, TSO – BR maroon, except *LNER teak. ● **Date:** 2019 ● **Service:** Loughborough Central to Leicester North ● **Location:** Rothley

BR '5MT' 4-6-0, BR lined black with late crests (Bachmann) + Stanier 'Black Five' 4-6-0, BR lined black with late crests (Hornby), BR Mk 1 RFO, RB, TSO, TSO, TSO, BCK – BR carmine and cream. ● **Date:** 2019 ● **Service:** Leicester North to Loughborough Central ● **Location:** Loughborough

LMS '8F' 2-8-0, BR black with early crests (Hornby), BR Mk 1 BCK, TSO, TSO, RB, TSO, BSK, SK*, BCK*, FK* - BR carmine and cream, except *BR chocolate and cream. ● **Date:** 2019 ● **Service:** Loughborough Central to Leicester North ● **Location:** Rothley

BR Class 33/1 Bo-Bo, BR blue (Heljan), BR Mk 1 BCK, TSO, TSO, RB, TSO, BSK – BR carmine and cream.
● **Date:** 2019 ● **Service:** Loughborough Central to Leicester North. ● **Location:** Quorn

SR air-smoothed 'Battle of Britain' 4-6-2, British Railways malachite green (Hornby), BR 20ton brake van, BR 12ton planked vent van, BR 12ton plywood vent van, BR 12ton planked vent van, three BR 12ton plywood vent vans, BR 12ton Shocvan, LNER 12ton non-vent van, BR 12ton planked vent van, BR 12ton plywood vent van, LMS 20ton brake van – BR bauxite. ● **Date:** 2017 ● **Service:** Demonstration freight ● **Location:** Loughborough Central

LNWR 'G2' 0-8-0, BR black with early crests (Bachmann), 15 16ton steel mineral open wagons, BR 20ton brake van* - BR grey, except *BR bauxite.
● **Date:** 2007 ● **Service:** GCR 'Windcutter' ● **Location:** Quorn

BR Class 55 Co-Co, BR two-tone green (Bachmann), BR MK 1 POS, POT, POS, POS, POT – Royal Mail red.
● **Date:** 2014 ● **Service:** TPO demonstration ● **Location:** Quorn

| USEFUL LINKS | |
|---|---|
| **Accurascale** | www.accurascale.co.uk |
| **Bachmann** | www.bachmann.co.uk |
| **Dapol** | www.dapol.co.uk |
| **Heljan** | www.heljan.dk |
| **Hornby** | www.hornby.com |
| **Oxford Rail** | www.oxfordrail.com |
| **Replica Railways** | www.replicarailways.co.uk |
| **The Model Centre (TMC)** | www.themodelcentre.com |

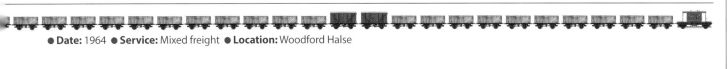

● **Date:** 1964 ● **Service:** Mixed freight ● **Location:** Woodford Halse

| SUITABLE 'OO' GAUGE FREIGHT ROLLING STOCK | | |
|---|---|---|
| **TYPE** | **LIVERY** | **MANUFACTURER** |
| 12ton BR fruit van | BR bauxite | Bachmann |
| 12ton BR banana van | BR bauxite | Dapol |
| 12ton GWR fruit van | BR bauxite | Bachmann |
| 12ton NE fruit van | BR bauxite | Bachmann |
| 12ton BR Pipe wagon | BR bauxite | Bachmann |
| 12ton BR Shocvan | BR bauxite | Bachmann |
| 12ton BR Shocbar open wagon | BR bauxite | Bachmann |
| 12ton BR vent van corrugated ends | BR bauxite | Bachmann |
| 12ton BR vent van planked | BR bauxite | Bachmann |
| 12ton BR vent van plywood | BR bauxite | Bachmann |
| 12ton LNER non-vent van | BR bauxite | Bachmann |
| 12ton SR vent van 2+2 planks | BR bauxite | Bachmann |
| 12ton SR vent van planked | BR bauxite | Bachmann |
| 12ton SR vent van plywood | BR bauxite | Bachmann |
| 12ton Insulfish Van | BR white/BR light blue | Hornby |
| 13ton high-sided steel open | BR bauxite | Bachmann |
| 14ton tank wagon | Shell/BP black | Bachmann |
| 16ton steel mineral open wagon | BR grey | Bachmann |
| 16ton slope-sided steel mineral open wagon | BR grey | Bachmann |
| 21ton steel mineral open wagon | BR grey | Hornby |
| 21ton hopper wagon | BR grey | Hornby |
| 22ton Plate wagon | BR grey | TMC/Bachmann |
| 22ton Tube wagon | BR bauxite | Bachmann |
| 24.5ton hopper wagon | BR grey | Accurascale |
| 27ton Iron ore tippler | BR grey | Bachmann/Hornby |
| BR 20ton brake van | BR grey/bauxite | Bachmann |
| BR 20ton brake van | BR grey/bauxite | Hornby |
| BR bogie bolster A wagon | BR grey | Bachmann |
| BR bogie bolster E wagon | BR bauxite | Dapol |
| BR 'Lowmac' wagon | BR bauxite | Hornby |
| BR 'Weltrol' wagon | BR grey/BR engineers' black | Bachmann |
| Conflat A wagon | BR bauxite | Bachmann |
| Conflat with AF container | BR bauxite | Bachmann |
| Conflat with BD container | BR bauxite | Bachmann |
| LMS 20ton brake van | BR grey/BR bauxite | Hornby |
| Midland Railway 20ton brake van | BR grey/BR bauxite | Bachmann |
| One-plank 'lowfit' open wagon | BR bauxite | Bachmann |
| Three-plank open wagon | BR bauxite | Bachmann |
| Five-plank open wagon | BR grey | Bachmann |
| Five-plank open wagon | BR bauxite | Hornby |
| Six-plank open wagon | BR grey | Oxford Rail |
| Seven-plank open wagon | BR grey | Bachmann |
| Nine-plank open wagon | BR grey | Hornby |

# THE
# PIRANHA
## PROJECT

**TIM SHACKLETON** scratchbuilds PNA ballast wagons, adding a welcome touch of variety to a rake of otherwise identical vehicles.

I ENJOY BUILDING WAGONS, either from kits or from scratch. With the availability of so much fine off the shelf rolling stock, this isn't the necessity it once was, so it's both a source of pleasure and a way of filling some of the remaining gaps in my fleet.

As a lineside observer of some 60 years standing, I enjoy looking at the subtle variations in the make-up of the freight trains that roll past me – whether it's a steam-age block train of 16ton mineral wagons or a modern intermodal,

it's highly unlikely that all the vehicles will be identical, even though the differences may be slight.

A case in point are these PNA ballast wagons, known unofficially as 'Piranhas'. Like most ballast opens they're heavily built but pretty unsophisticated in design. There are five basic versions, superficially similar but differing significantly in detail. Bachmann offers splendid models of the two most numerous types, which also happen to share a common underframe with its popular TTA tank wagon, but on a train of any length (and from what I can tell, PNAs have only ever operated in block formation) you need a bit more variety.

These scratchbuilds are the outcome – basically a set of styrene boxes with a lot of external ribbing, running on equally simple underframes for which no ready-to-run source exists. The only tricky bits are the suspension pedestals, for which I used Cambrian mouldings. Buffers are bought in, but apart from a few brake-gear castings pretty well everything else was cut from styrene strip and sheet.

The aim here is to show you that scratchbuilding needn't be at all difficult. It's just like building a kit except you start a couple of stages further back in the process. I've been doing it for more than 50 years now and the first thing I discovered was how straightforward it all was. The second was how exciting it is to have a model that no one else owns. Obviously, you get better with practice, but the hardest part is probably making a start. Because I know how much enjoyment scratchbuilding can afford, this is never a problem. ■

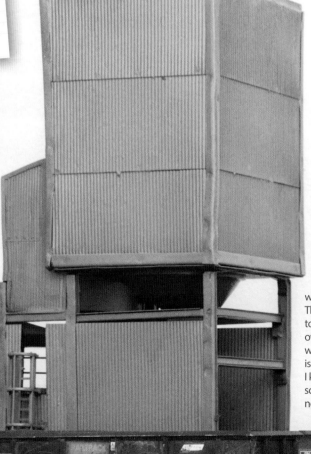

**The completed PNA wagons stand in a world of white – typical of the loading facilities that these low height open wagons use.**

## STEP BY STEP SCRATCHBUILDING PIRANHA BALLAST WAGONS FOR 'OO'

Intermediate
**SKILL LEVEL**
Beginner Advanced

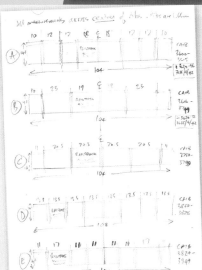

**1** This is how most of my scratchbuilding projects start out – a simple dimensioned sketch showing the major bodywork variations. Some modellers like to prepare exquisitely detailed drawings which I'm sure is a very satisfying thing to do but it's no more a guarantee of accuracy than my homespun method.

**2** Basic shells are made out of 30 thou styrene sheet. I use Plastruct or Evergreen plastic materials depending on their availability. The Maquette range supplied via Albion Hobbies is an equally useful source of plastic section and sheet.

**3** I use a lot of Evergreen styrene sections in my modelling but the correct sizes for what I need aren't always available. For the bracing along the tops of the bodywork, I made a simple jig in which I could file a triangular shape from square-section 80thou strip.

**4** I made the triangular bracing pieces overlength and then, once the solvent had evaporated, I cut mitred ends using a circular saw attachment in a minidrill.

**5** Gaps are inevitable but Squadron Green Putty is easy to work and dries quickly. I've tried a fair few fillers in my time, but this is the one that works best for me.

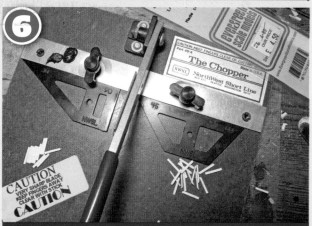

**6** I needed to make dozens of bracing strips for the wagon sides, using 0.40 x 0.60 Evergreen strip. To ensure consistency, the guillotine-like North West Short Line 'Chopper' is invaluable. Some will inevitably be slightly over-length but they can be trimmed back.

STEP BY STEP **SCRATCHBUILDING PIRANHA BALLAST WAGONS FOR 'OO'**

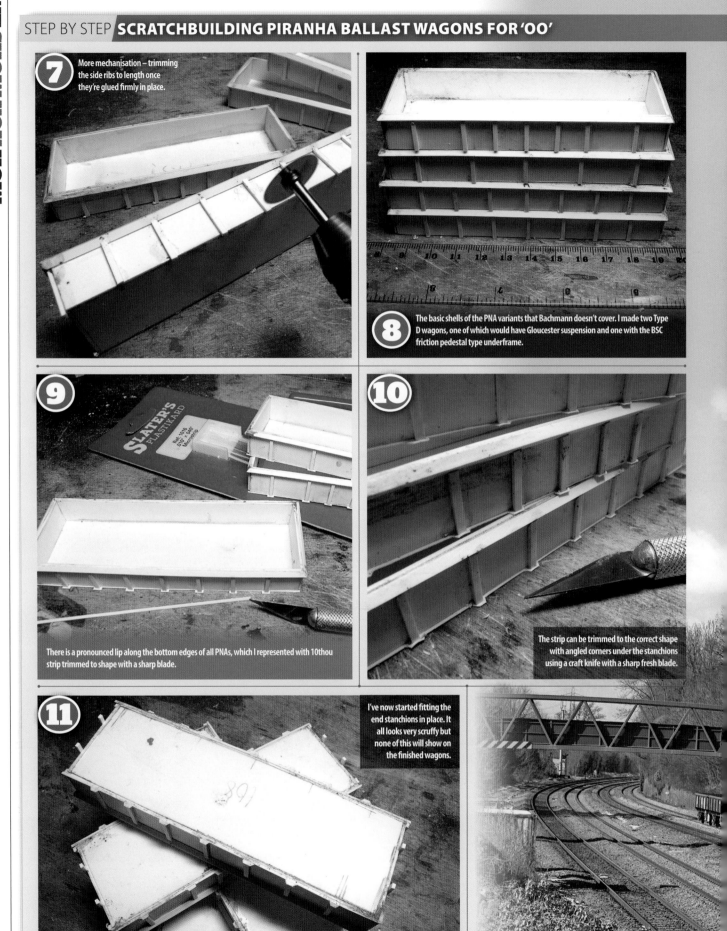

**7** More mechanisation – trimming the side ribs to length once they're glued firmly in place.

**8** The basic shells of the PNA variants that Bachmann doesn't cover. I made two Type D wagons, one of which would have Gloucester suspension and one with the BSC friction pedestal type underframe.

**9** There is a pronounced lip along the bottom edges of all PNAs, which I represented with 10thou strip trimmed to shape with a sharp blade.

**10** The strip can be trimmed to the correct shape with angled corners under the stanchions using a craft knife with a sharp fresh blade.

**11** I've now started fitting the end stanchions in place. It all looks very scruffy but none of this will show on the finished wagons.

Intermediate

Beginner **SKILL LEVEL** Advanced

⑫

Solebars are made from U-section styrene, 3.25mm deep and set 23mm apart back to back. It's essential to get them square and parallel or running may be compromised.

⑬

There are weld lines on the inside of the body, corresponding to the ribbing on the outside. You could draw them on with a pencil – I've done this before – but it looks more effective if you make them out of 0.33mm brass wire. I made another little jig to make sure I cut them to the right length.

PNA wagons are still in regular service on the national network. On March 19 2018 Class 50 50008 *Thunderer* passes Barrow Upon Soar on the Midland Main Line with 6Z50 – the 12.29 Chaddesden Sidings-Wembley Euro Freight Operations Centre consisting of 11 empty PNAs.
Paul Biggs.

WE SHOW YOU HOW

STEP BY STEP **SCRATCHBUILDING PIRANHA BALLAST WAGONS FOR 'OO'**

Intermediate
Beginner **SKILL LEVEL** Advanced

**14** None of this has been particularly strenuous so far and we are beginning to see something that resembles a batch of PNA ballast wagons, each of them different. The next stage will be to spray-paint the bodyshells. Phoenix Precision's 'Freightliner Green' is a good match.

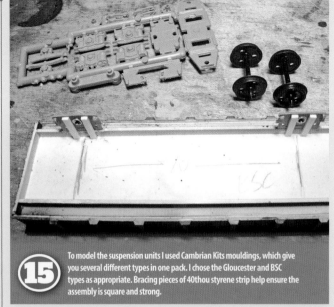

**15** To model the suspension units I used Cambrian Kits mouldings, which give you several different types in one pack. I chose the Gloucester and BSC types as appropriate. Bracing pieces of 40thou styrene strip help ensure the assembly is square and strong.

**16** Be very careful when aligning the axles – they need to be true and parallel in every plane. Once satisfied with their alignment, leave for a good 24 hours for the adhesives to cure properly. In the meantime you can make a little styrene box to contain the Liquid Lead that I use as ballast to increase the wagons' weight.

**17** The bottom of the ballast box is made from scrap styrene, solidly glued in place so none of the lead can escape.

**18** The tough-looking Oleo-pneumatic buffers are white metal castings from Lanarkshire Model Supplies, reference BP03 and BP04.

**19** Coupling hooks and instanters are by Masokits, plain links made by hand using 0.45 wire. I find the mass production of such items to be relaxing and therapeutic. I will often make five or six pairs of working screw couplings in one hit.

The Piranha wagons are used for the transport of ballast by Network Rail. These scratchbuilt models have been loaded with fresh ballast for transport to the next engineering site.

**20** The triangular strengtheners between body and solebar are made from mass-produced sections of 15thou strip glued in place with Limonene. As you can see, there are quite a lot of them. The square notch is to accommodate the upper lip of the solebar.

**21** Now we can start to add the underframe detail, remembering that each individual diagram is subtly different. The brake wheels (linked by 40thou plastic rod) are Cambrian, the brake valves and cylinders by S Kits.

**22** A different arrangement of brake gear on one of the five-rib wagons. I made the brake lever from brass strip left over from an etched kit.

**23** This seven-rib wagon is different again. It has clasp brakes and the brake cylinder is mounted centrally. So much for standardisation.

| KEY MATERIALS | |
|---|---|
| Shells | 30thou plastic sheet |
| Top rib | 80thou square section plastic filed triangular |
| Side ribs | 0.40 x 0.60 plastic section |
| Bottom edge | 0.10 x 0.40 and 0.20 x 0.40 plastic section |
| Solebars | 40 thou with U plastic section |
| Inner weld lines | 0.33 brass wire |
| Tough-looking buffers | Lanarkshire Models (Cat No. BP03 and BP04) |
| Suspension units | Cambrian Models (Cat No. C40 2) |
| Solebar/body triangular ribs | 0.15 thou strip |

| USEFUL LINKS | |
|---|---|
| Cambrian Models | www.cambrianmodelrail.co.uk |
| Lanarkshire Models | www.lanarkshiremodels.com |
| Deluxe Materials | www.deluxematerials.co.uk |
| Squadron Green Putty | www.squadron.com |

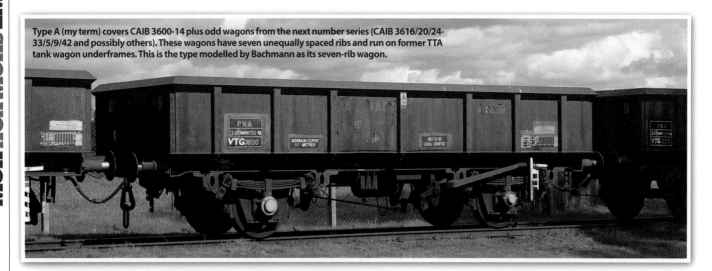

Type A (my term) covers CAIB 3600-14 plus odd wagons from the next number series (CAIB 3616/20/24-33/5/9/42 and possibly others). These wagons have seven unequally spaced ribs and run on former TTA tank wagon underframes. This is the type modelled by Bachmann as its seven-rib wagon.

# PNA Variations

**A**LTHOUGH ALL PNAs superficially look much the same, there are five different body styles, depending on the dimensions of the donor chassis. For simplicity I'm using letters of the alphabet to distinguish between the five types rather than official diagram numbers. The only consistent factors are the external height of the bodysides (14.1mm in 4mm scale) and the width of the bodyside ribs (1.65mm). The clear section of the bodysides (between the hefty top strengthener and the fine web at the bottom) is 11mm deep. Martyn Read's excellent photographs show the differences far better than words.

Type B also has a TTA-type underframe but the bodies (which are the same length as Type A) have five unequally-spaced ribs. This is the biggest single group of PNAs, numbered 3615-3749 minus the wagons mentioned above, which were numbered out of the sequence in the first series. This is Bachmann's five-rib wagon.

Type C (CAIB 3750-99) has BSC friction pedestal suspension and five equally spaced ribs. They're slightly shorter than A and B, and no ready-to-run model exists.

Type D (CAIB 3800-28) has Gloucester suspension (quite a few have BSC with disc brakes) and are longer than any of the other PNAs. They have seven evenly spaced ribs.

Type E (3829-49) has seven unevenly spaced ribs arranged in a different pattern to A, and they're slightly shorter too. They have Gloucester suspension, some with disc brakes.

You can't have too many close-up details. The work that people such as Martyn Read do in recording freight stock is invaluable. Without them, we wouldn't have a fraction of the high-quality reference material that's readily available online. Try *ukrailwaypics. smugmug.com* for starters.

# Forward to 2021

An astonishing 172 new model projects are in development from expression of interest to nearing delivery. **MIKE WILD** looks ahead to 2021 and beyond and the next projects which are being planned and produced across 'OO', 'OO9', 'N' and 'O' gauge.

InterCity APT

370 006

The Hornby 'OO' gauge APT has reached the first engineering sample stage. Expect it in the shops in 2021.

Hornby is making an all-new model of the iconic Class 370 APT for 'OO' gauge. In 1983 a test train lead by 370006 leaves Carlisle.
Colin Whitfield/Railphotoprints.co.uk.

**T**HE END OF 2020 is within sight. With 2021 just around the corner we are looking forward to another year of exciting model railway releases – and what a list we have with the chance of more than 170 new items across locomotives, carriages and wagons and 'OO', 'OO9', 'N' and 'O' gauge.

The range of products on offer never ceases to amaze us each year as we come to put together this annual feature for the *Hornby Magazine Yearbook*, and this year is certainly no exception. Whatever era, period or region you model there is something for you in this list, though in the case of the early period there is a possibility it might be in a different scale to what you model. Nevertheless, the choice is near endless with a massive 89 locomotive projects and 83 carriage and wagon models on the table.

As with our Forward to 2020 feature there are a number of items which have never made it onto our listing including Hornby's Stephenson's *Rocket* which was announced in January 2020 and released the same month and the EFE Rail Class 17, announced and delivered in August 2020, but there are plenty of new additions too. However, the past year has seen a rise in 'expressions of interest' from manufacturers where potential customers are invited to show whether they would like to see a model produced in ready-to-run form. This is good on the one hand in that it shows what might be possible, but unfortunately there are projects which don't gain the support they need in order to move forward. Those that are 'expression of interest' models in this survey are listed as TBC (To Be Confirmed) in our tables to differentiate from those where the delivery date is To Be Announced, as in all the latter cases significant progress is already being made in the development process.

This year has seen a rise in the total number of locomotive projects by five with 10 more items in the 'OO' gauge listing than in 2020 while the 'OO9' list has stayed static and both 'N' and 'O' gauge have seen reductions in their list of future projects by two and three respectively. There are also several models which are on the horizon. In fact, by the time you read this the Bachmann Midland '1P' 0-4-4T and Dapol

Ellis Clark Trains is working on a ready-to-run Presflo cement hopper for 'O' gauge.

| TABLE 1 - 'OO' GAUGE NEW RELEASES FOR – 2020/2021-ONWARDS | | | |
|---|---|---|---|
| **CLASS** | **REGION** | **MANUFACTURER** | **EXPECTED** |
| GWR steam railmotor | Western | Kernow MRC | TBA |
| GWR 'Large Prairie' 2-6-2T | Western | Dapol | 2021 |
| GWR '63XX' 2-6-0 | Western | Dapol | 2020 |
| GWR 'Manor' 4-6-0 | Western | Dapol | TBA |
| GWR '94XX' 0-6-0PT | Western | Bachmann | 2020 |
| SECR 'D' 4-4-0 | Southern | Locomotion/Rails/Dapol | 2021 |
| SR Bulleid Leader | Southern | KR Models | TBC |
| Caledonian '812' 0-6-0 | Scottish | Rails of Sheffield/Bachmann | 2021 |
| Midland '1P' 0-4-4T | Midland | Bachmann | 2020 |
| NER petrol railcar | Eastern | Rails of Sheffield/Heljan | 2020 |
| LNER 'A2/2' 4-6-2 | Eastern | Hornby | 2021 |
| LNER 'A2/3' 4-6-2 | Eastern | Hornby | 2021 |
| NER 'J26' 0-6-0 | Eastern | Oxford Rail | TBA |
| NER 'J27' 0-6-0 | Eastern | Oxford Rail | 2020 |
| LNER 'G5' 0-4-4T | Eastern | TMC/Bachmann | TBA |
| LNER 'V2' 2-6-2 | Eastern | Bachmann | 2021 |
| LNER 'W1' 4-6-4 (original) | Eastern | Hornby | 2021 |
| LNER 'W1' 4-6-4 (rebuilt) | Eastern | Hornby | 2021 |
| BR '2MT' 2-6-0 | Various | Hornby | 2021 |
| GT3 gas turbine 4-6-0 | Midland | KR Models | 2020 |
| Brown Boveri gas turbine, 18000 | Western | Rails of Sheffield/Heljan | 2020 |
| 'Fell' diesel 10100 | Midland | KR Models | 2021 |
| DHP1 prototype Bo-Bo | Midland | KR Models | TBC |
| Class 02 | Various | Heljan | TBA |
| Class 20/3 | Various | Bachmann | 2020 |
| Class 25/1 | Various | Bachmann | TBA |
| Class 25/2 | Various | Bachmann | TBA |
| Class 25/3 | Various | Heljan | 2020 |
| Class 37/0 | Various | Accurascale | 2021 |
| Class 37/4 (modern era) | Various | Accurascale | 2021 |
| Class 37/6 | Various | Accurascale | 2021 |
| Class 45/0 | Midland/Eastern | Heljan | 2021 |
| Class 45/1 | Midland/Eastern | Heljan | 2021 |
| Class 47 | Various | Heljan | 2021 |
| Class 55 | Eastern | Accurascale | 2021 |
| Class 59 | Western | Dapol | 2021 |
| Class 73/9 | Scottish/Southern | KMS/Accurascale | TBC |
| Class 86/0 | Midland | Heljan | 2020 |
| Class 86/4 | Midland | Heljan | 2021 |
| Class 89 | Eastern | Rails/Accurascale | TBC |
| Class 91 | Eastern | Hornby | 2021 |
| Class 92 | Various | Accurascale | 2021 |
| GWR AEC railcar | Western | Heljan | 2020 |
| Class 142 | Midland/Eastern | Realtrack | TBA |
| Class 168 | Chiltern | Bachmann | TBA |
| Class 170/171 | Various | Bachmann | TBA |
| Class 370 APT | Midland | Hornby | 2021 |
| Class 410 4-BEP | Southern | Bachmann | 2021 |
| LT 1938 tube stock | London Transport | EFE Rail | 2021 |
| **Total: 49** | **Steam: 19** | **Diesel/electric: 30** | |

Below: **Minerva Models is continuing development of its 'O' gauge Class 14. Decoration samples are expected before the end of the year.**

'43XX' 2-6-0 for 'OO' and Graham Farish '8F' 2-8-0 are expected in the shops across November and early December. Heljan too is set to release its 'OO' gauge GWR AEC railcar before the end of 2020 while 'O' gauge should see the Bogie Bolster 'E' from Dapol and potentially, if all goes to plan, either the Class 17 or GWR AEC railcar from Heljan for the same scale.

## 'OO' gauge

The most popular gauge in ready-to-run British outline continues to flourish with new announcements on a near monthly basis of one level or another. Hornby has led the way in 2020 with a strong range of announcements in its annual catalogue to celebrate its centenary year covering the Gresley 'W1' 4-6-4, LNER 'A2/2' and 'A2/3' 4-6-2s, BR '2MT' 2-6-0, Class 91 overhead electric and even a brand-new model of the iconic Class 370 Advanced Passenger Train. This impressive crop of new announcements are also being joined by an extension of the BR Mk 1 range by the addition of the Restaurant Buffet and, even more exciting, the 'Coronation Scot' carriages to go with its 2018 released streamlined Stanier 'Princess Coronation' 4-6-2s.

Bachmann has expanded its portfolio with the addition of the EFE Rail brand with its most compelling 'OO' gauge new item being a motorised version of the popular EFE 1938 London Transport tube stock. This upgraded version of the previously static EFE product will feature directional lighting, decoder socket and a motor bogie for the first time in its existence. Final decoration amendments were being made in October with release expected in winter 2021.

In addition, while Bachmann has

Next in for 'OO' gauge from Heljan is its all-new GWR AEC railcar. It will be joined by an 'O' gauge model of the same railcar with six liveries available in each scale.

Accurascale has added a series of Class 37 models to its plans with the first due for release in the second quarter of 2021. The fleet models the Class 37/0, 37/4 and 37/6 sub-classes providing missing links in 'OO' gauge.

Next for release by Accurascale are its PTA/JUA/JTA tippler wagons in a choice of stone and iron ore liveries for 'OO' gauge.

had a busy year of new releases (see pages 70-79), there are still more exciting projects on the way in the near future including the GWR '94XX' 0-6-0PT, 'V2' 2-6-2, Class 20/3 and its all-new models of the Class 25 family for 'OO' too. In the carriage and wagon section it also has the promised new range of Bulleid main line 63ft corridor stock on the cards alongside the VEA box van and a commission from TMC to produce the BR 24.5ton mineral wagon.

Accurascale has been growing its portfolio greatly over the past 12 months. Following on from its Class 92 and 'Deltic' announcements it added a series of Class 37s to its future plans covering the original Class 37/0s, modern era Class 37s and Class 37/6s (including Network Rail operated 97201). The specification is outstanding for all these locomotives and with the high calibre of its freight wagons we are all eagerly looking forward to the first of its locomotives arriving. World events have caused some delays, but it looks like the second quarter of 2021 will be busy for Accurascale's locomotive department.

Concurrently, Accurascale has continued with production of freight stock with the JSA steel coil carrier joining its PTA/JUA family (with which they shared running gear) as well as further announcements for more modern coal and biomass hoppers too. Plus there is the imposing KUA 16-wheel nuclear flask wagon to look forward to as well in early 2021.

Dapol has eaten away at its list of projects progressively during 2020 leaving just five for 'OO' gauge on

Heljan's new 'OO' Class 25 is progressing well and will be entering production soon for release this winter.

Bachmann's new EFE Rail brand is making a ready-to-run motorised version of the EFE 1938 tube stock for 'OO' – a product which has been long requested.

Kernow Model Rail Centre has moved forward with its LSWR Road Van for 'OO' gauge. This is the first engineering sample.

the table. Three are Western Region steam locomotives and the first of those, the '43XX' 2-6-0, was close to arrival as we closed for press in late October. Also in development are the GWR 'Large Prairie' 2-6-2T, 'Manor' 4-6-0, Class 59 heavy freight diesel-electric and O&K bogie stone hopper in Yeoman livery – the latter due to arrive in December 2020.

Meanwhile Heljan has been working towards a triumphant return to the 'OO' gauge market with five locomotive projects in varying stages of development. The first to be released will be its GWR AEC railcar in six liveries which is set to be followed by its new Class 86/0 and then the Class 25/3 over the winter. Its Class 45 and 47 models are slated for release later in 2021.

Beyond the big names there is plenty to look forward to. Rails of Sheffield has been busy working with Dapol to produce the Wainwright 'D' 4-4-0 in 'OO' gauge

in collaboration with Locomotion Models together with Heljan on the NER Petrol Electric Autocar and unique Brown Boveri gas turbine 18000 with Heljan. All three are expected to be available in the first half of 2021. Also worth mentioning is that Rails has an expression of interest form open for a potential project with Accurascale to make the unique

Class 89 AC electric in 'OO'.

Hattons doesn't have a 'OO' locomotive project in the listings this year, but it does have an impressive collection of four and six-wheel carriages on the way for release in the second quarter of 2021.

KR Models, which started its business with a crowd-funded model of gas turbine prototype GT3, is now working on three further locomotives as well as the Consett iron ore bogie hoppers. Its next locomotive after GT3 will be the 'Fell' 2-D-2 diesel-electric which is already at the first sample stage while it has expressions of interest open for the Bulleid Leader and Clayton prototype DHP1.

## 'OO9' narrow gauge

It has been a quiet year for narrow gauge ready-to-run with just one project from last year's list being completed and no new

announcements. We are currently waiting to hear updates on the Bachmann 'Quarry Hunslet' as well as the Kato produced Peco George England 0-4-0STT and Double Fairlie locomotives from the Ffestiniog Railway.

## 'N' gauge

Similarly, 'N' gauge has had a steady year in 2020 with the arrival of four new locomotives (including the soon to arrive Stanier '8F' 2-8-0 from Graham Farish) while announcements have been few and far between.

Revolution Trains is the most prolific in the launches phase with a number of projects pending a decision following closure of the expression of interest phase including the Class 89 and APT-E. However, there is good news as its currently developing projects are approaching the final stages including the Class 92 and Class 321 EMU while several of its 'N'

Bachmann's new 'OO' gauge Class 20/3 is expected in late 2020 or early 2021.

Rails of Sheffield and manufacturing partner Heljan have been working on a highly detailed model of the NER Petrol Electric Autocar for 'OO'.

gauge wagons are expected in 2021 including the Class A tanker, Cemflo cement tanker and Ecofret container flats.

Equally enticing for modern image modellers is the impending arrival of the Graham Farish Class 319 EMU for the scale while the manufacturer is also continuing its work on the refurbished Class 31 for 'N' gauge to expand its appeal and livery options.

Dapol's current projects are focused on the Bulleid 'Light Pacifics' as well as a collection of Maunsell high-window corridor stock with arrival dates on both to be confirmed in late October 2020.

## TABLE 2 – 'OO' GAUGE NEW CARRIAGE AND WAGON IN DEVELOPMENT – 2020/2021-ONWARDS

| VEHICLE | REGION | MANUFACTURER | EXPECTED |
|---|---|---|---|
| LMR four-wheel open third coach | Midland | Hornby | 2021 |
| Four-wheel four-compartment coach | Various | Hattons | 2021 |
| Four-wheel five-compartment coach | Various | Hattons | 2021 |
| Four-wheel brake coach | Various | Hattons | 2021 |
| Six-wheel four-compartment coach | Various | Hattons | 2021 |
| Six-wheel five-compartment coach | Various | Hattons | 2021 |
| Six-wheel brake coach | Various | Hattons | 2021 |
| Six-wheel full brake | Various | Hattons | 2021 |
| SR Bulleid 63ft Semi open Brake Third | Southern | Bachmann | TBA |
| SR Bulleid 63ft Corridor Composite | Southern | Bachmann | TBA |
| SR Bulleid 63ft Corridor Third | Southern | Bachmann | TBA |
| SR Bulleid 63ft Brake Composite | Southern | Bachmann | TBA |
| SR Inspection Saloon, *Caroline* | Southern | Revolution Trains | 2021 |
| LMS 'Coronation' 65ft RFO | Midland | Hornby | 2021 |
| LMS 'Coronation' 57ft FK | Midland | Hornby | 2021 |
| LMS 'Coronation' 57ft RTO | Midland | Hornby | 2021 |
| LMS 'Coronation' 57ft BFK | Midland | Hornby | 2021 |
| LMS 'Coronation' 50ft RK | Midland | Hornby | 2021 |
| BR Mk 1 RB/RBR | Various | Hornby | 2020 |
| Trans-Pennine Mk 5 carriage sets | Midland/Eastern | Accurascale | 2021 |
| Caledonian Sleeper Mk 5 carriages | Midland | Accurascale | 2021 |
| LSWR road van | Southern | Kernow Model Rail Centre | TBA |
| SECR 16ton covered goods wagon | Southern | Rails of Sheffield | 2021 |
| Consett iron ore bogie wagon | Eastern | KR Models | 2021 |
| BR 24.5ton mineral wagon | Various | TMC/Bachmann | TBA |
| BR 'Salmon' engineers flat | Various | Flangeway | 2020 |
| Plasser 12ton GPC crane | Various | Hattons Originals | 2021 |
| FWA Ecofret container flats | Various | Revolution Trains | 2021 |
| HAA coal hopper | Various | Accurascale | TBA |
| HAA coal hopper | Various | KMS/Trains 4U/Cavalex | TBA |
| CDA china clay hopper | Various | KMS/Trains 4U/Cavalex | TBA |
| HYA/IIA bogie coal hopper | Various | Accurascale | 2021 |
| IIA biomass hopper | Various | Accurascale | 2021 |
| IPA car carriers | Various | Accurascale | 2021 |
| HOA hopper wagon | Various | Revolution Trains | TBA |
| KFA 'Warflat' | Various | Trains 4U/Cavalex | 2021 |
| KUA nuclear flask wagon | Various | Accurascale | 2020 |
| IWA Holdall bogie vans | Various | Revolution Trains | TBA |
| IWA timber carrier | Various | Revolution Trains | TBA |
| IZA Cargowaggon twins | Various | Kernow Model Rail Centre | 2020 |
| JGA bogie aggregate wagon | Various | Cavalex Models | TBA |
| JHA O&K aggregate hopper | Western | Dapol | 2020 |
| JSA steel coil carrier | Western | Accurascale | 2021 |
| PTA/JTA/JUA bogie wagon | Various | Accurascale | 2020 |
| TEA 100ton tanker | Various | Cavalex Models | 2021 |
| VEA four-wheel van | Various | Bachmann | TBA |
| **Total:** 45 | | | |

## TABLE 3 – 'OO9' NARROW GAUGE NEW ROLLING STOCK IN DEVELOPMENT – 2020/2021-ONWARDS

| CLASS | REGION | MANUFACTURER | EXPECTED |
|---|---|---|---|
| Quarry Hunslet 0-4-0ST | Industrial | Bachmann | TBA |
| Baguley-Drewry 4wDM | Industrial | Bachmann | TBA |
| L&B Baldwin 2-4-2T | L&B | Heljan | 2020 |
| England 0-4-0STT | Ffestiniog | Peco/Kato | 2021 |
| Double Fairlie 0-4-4-0T | Ffestiniog | Peco/Kato | TBC |
| Ashover Light Railway carriage | Narrow gauge | Bachmann | TBA |
| RNAD open wagon | Narrow gauge | Bachmann | TBA |
| RNAD flat wagon | Narrow gauge | Bachmann | TBA |
| RNAD box van | Narrow gauge | Bachmann | TBA |
| RNAD brake van | Narrow gauge | Bachmann | TBA |
| **Total:** 10 | | | |

## TABLE 4 – 'N' GAUGE NEW LOCOMOTIVES IN DEVELOPMENT – 2020/2021-ONWARDS

| CLASS | REGION | MANUFACTURER | EXPECTED |
|---|---|---|---|
| GWR '56XX' 0-6-2T | Western | Sonic Models | 2020 |
| SR 'West Country' 4-6-2 | Southern | Dapol | TBA |
| SR rebuilt 'West Country' 4-6-2 | Southern | Dapol | TBA |
| LMS '8F' 2-8-0 | Midland | Graham Farish | 2020 |
| LMS Beyer-Garratt 2-6-0+0-6-2 | Midland | Hattons | TBC |
| Hunslet 0-6-0DM | Industrial | N Gauge Society | 2020 |
| Class 31 (refurbished) | Various | Graham Farish | 2020 |
| Class 89 | Eastern | Revolution Trains | TBC |
| Class 92 | Various | Revolution Trains | 2020 |
| Class 158 | Various | Graham Farish | TBA |
| Class 319 | Midland/Southern | Graham Farish | TBA |
| Class 321 | Midland/Eastern | Revolution Trains | TBA |
| Class 800 | Western/Eastern | Kato | TBA |
| APT-E | Midland | Revolution Trains | TBC |
| **Total:** 14 | **Steam:** 5 | **Diesel:** 11 | |

## TABLE 5 – 'N' GAUGE NEW CARRIAGE AND WAGON IN DEVELOPMENT – 2020/2021-ONWARDS

| VEHICLE | REGION | MANUFACTURER | EXPECTED |
|---|---|---|---|
| SR Maunsell high-window First | Southern | Dapol | TBA |
| SR Maunsell high-window Second | Southern | Dapol | TBA |
| SR Maunsell high-window Composite | Southern | Dapol | TBA |
| SR Maunsell high-window Brake | Southern | Dapol | TBA |
| SR Inspection Saloon *Caroline* | Southern | Revolution Trains | TBA |
| BR Mk 3 sleeping car | Various | Dapol | 2020 |
| Trans Pennine Mk 5 carriage sets | Midland/Eastern | Revolution Trains | 2021 |
| Caledonian Sleeper Mk 5 carriages | Midland | Revolution Trains | 2021 |
| Cemflo cement tanker | Southern/Eastern | Revolution/Accurascale | 2021 |
| Class A 35ton tanker | Various | Revolution Trains | 2021 |
| FWA Ecofret container flats | Various | Revolution Trains | 2021 |
| IWA Holdall bogie vans | Various | Revolution Trains | TBA |
| IWA timber carrier | Various | Revolution Trains | TBA |
| MTV/Zander open wagon | Various | Revolution Trains | 2021 |
| MNA/JNA bogie open wagons | Various | Revolution Trains | TBA |
| PFA coal container flats | Various | Revolution Trains | TBA |
| **Total:** 16 | | | |

Hornby's Thompson 'A2/2' and 'A2/3' 4-6-2s will be released in 2021 modelling both the rebuilds from the 'P2' 2-8-2s and the new build locomotives for 'OO'.

In 'N' gauge modern wagons are holding sway at Revolution Trains including this Ecofret container flats.

| THE HEADLINES - ENGINES | | | | | |
|---|---|---|---|---|---|
| **Planned '00' gauge new locomotives** | | | | | |
| | 2017 | 2018 | 2019 | 2020 | 2021 |
| Steam: | 21 | 15 | 18 | 14 | 19 |
| Diesel: | 25 | 23 | 23 | 25 | 30 |
| Total: | 46 | 38 | 42 | 39 | 49 |
| **Planned '009' narrow gauge locomotives** | | | | | |
| | | | | 2020 | 2021 |
| Steam: | | | | 4 | 4 |
| Diesel: | | | | 1 | 1 |
| Total: | | | | 5 | 5 |
| **Planned 'N' gauge new locomotives** | | | | | |
| | 2017 | 2018 | 2019 | 2020 | 2021 |
| Steam: | 9 | 10 | 9 | 5 | 5 |
| Diesel: | 14 | 16 | 15 | 11 | 11 |
| Total: | 23 | 26 | 24 | 16 | 14 |
| **Planned 'O' gauge new locomotives** | | | | | |
| | 2017 | 2018 | 2019 | 2020 | 2021 |
| Steam: | 9 | 8 | 7 | 6 | 3 |
| Diesel: | 11 | 11 | 14 | 18 | 18 |
| Total: | 20 | 18 | 21 | 24 | 21 |
| Overall: | 87 | 82 | 87 | 84 | 89 |

| TABLE 6 - 'O' GAUGE NEW RELEASES – 2020/2021-ONWARDS | | | |
|---|---|---|---|
| **CLASS** | **REGION** | **MANUFACTURER** | **EXPECTED** |
| GWR '45XX' 2-6-2T | Western | Lionheart Trains/Dapol | 2021 |
| GWR '2251' 0-6-0 | Western | Heljan | TBA |
| LMS 'Black Five' 4-6-0 | Midland | Ellis Clark/Darstaed | 2021 |
| Class 02 | Various | Heljan | 2021 |
| Class 09 | Southern | Gaugemaster/Dapol | TBA |
| Class 14 | Western | Minerva | 2021 |
| Class 17 | Eastern/Scottish | Heljan | 2020 |
| Class 26 | Eastern/Scottish | Heljan | 2021 |
| Class 31/1 | Various | Heljan | 2020 |
| Class 31/4 | Various | Heljan | 2021 |
| Class 40, centre headcode | Midland/Eastern | Heljan | 2021 |
| Class 43 HST | Various | KMS Railtech/Cavalex | TBC |
| Class 47 | Various | Heljan | 2021 |
| Class 56 | Midland/Eastern | Heljan | 2021 |
| Class 66 | All | Dapol | TBA |
| Class 117 | Western/Midland | Heljan | TBA |
| Class 121 | Western/Midland | Heljan | TBA |
| Class 121 | Western/Midland | Dapol | 2020 |
| Class 122 | Western/Midland | Heljan | TBA |
| Class 122 | Western/Midland | Dapol | 2020 |
| GWR AEC railcar | Western | Heljan | 2020 |
| **Total: 21** | **Steam: 3** | **Diesel: 18** | |

Hornby's 2020 range 'OO' gauge 'Hush Hush' 4-6-4s are due to be released in the first quarter of 2021 covering the original and rebuilt styling of the unique locomotive.

The KUA 16-wheel nuclear flask carrier is approaching release with Accurascale for 'OO'.

New to Hornby's collection of Mk 1s is the Restaurant Buffet. Delivery is expected in late 2020.

## 'O' gauge

7mm scale has seen an overall reduction in the number of expected models by three through continued delivery of new models in late 2019 and 2020, but there is still plenty to look forward to. Perhaps the most surprising announcement of the year came at Model Rail Scotland when KMS Railtech opened expressions of interest for an 'O' gauge HST covering the power cars and Mk 3 trailer coaches.

Heljan remains at the centre of ready-to-run in this scale with its project list featuring the Class 02 (newly announced in late September 2020), 17, 26 (newly announced in late October), Class 31/1 and 31/4, centre-headcode Class 40, Class 47, 56, 117, 121, 122 and AEC railcar. All those projects are expected to be realised over the next 12 months with most

now having reached, at least, engineering samples. The next arrival is expected to be the GWR AEC railcar which will be followed by the Class 31s and then the Class 17s, the latter potentially in the first quarter of 2021.

Heljan has also committed to a new range of BR Mk 2/a carriages for 'O' gauge modelling the Tourist Second Open, First Corridor, Brake Second Open and Brake First Corridor in a variety of liveries

The Rails, Locomotion and Dapol collaboration is working towards release of its model of the Wainwright 'D' 4-4-0 for 'OO' gauge. Decoration samples have been received and a release date is to be announced.

from BR blue and grey to Regional Railways and Network SouthEast. They will also be designed to accept drop in battery powered light bars.

Other locomotives to look forward to include Dapol's project to produce a ready-to-run Class 66 for 'O' gauge as well as the hotly anticipated Ellis Clark Trains Stanier 'Black Five' 4-6-0.

On the rolling stock front Ellis Clark is also busy with development of its collection of Thompson carriages and now its first wagon – the BR Presflo cement hopper for 7mm scale which promises a highly detailed injection moulded body and many separately fitted parts.

We can also look forward to

a collection of Stroudley four-wheel carriages from Dapol in 'O' gauge together with its Bogie Bolster 'E' and BR Conflat wagon too, all of which fill important gaps in the steam era for passenger and freight stock

## Overview

2020 may have had its challenges for model manufacturers due to the global pandemic, but on reflection it hasn't stopped anything. Some models may be a little later than originally planned, but that may be a good thing for our wallets. There is so much to look forward to in 2021 and it will make the next 12 months just as exciting as ever as we keep you up to date with the latest news and arrivals through *Hornby Magazine*.

Keep your eyes on *Hornby Magazine* and *www.keymodelworld. com* to see the latest model announcements as they happen. ∎

| TABLE 7 – 'O' GAUGE NEW CARRIAGE AND WAGON IN DEVELOPMENT – 2020/2021-ONWARDS | | | |
|---|---|---|---|
| VEHICLE | REGION | MANUFACTURER | EXPECTED |
| LBSCR Stroudley four-wheel carriages | Southern | Dapol | 2021 |
| LNER Gresley Open Third | Eastern | Hattons Model Railways | 2021 |
| LNER Gresley Corridor Third | Eastern | Hattons Model Railways | 2021 |
| LNER Gresley Brake Composite | Eastern | Hattons Model Railways | 2021 |
| LNER Thompson Full Brake | Eastern | Ellis Clark/Darstaed | 2021 |
| LNER Thompson Corridor Third | Eastern | Ellis Clark/Darstaed | 2021 |
| LNER Thompson Restaurant Third Open | Eastern | Ellis Clark/Darstaed | 2021 |
| LNER Thompson Restaurant First Kitchen | Eastern | Ellis Clark/Darstaed | 2021 |
| LNER Thompson Corridor First | Eastern | Ellis Clark/Darstaed | 2021 |
| LNER Thompson Brake Corridor Third | Eastern | Ellis Clark/Darstaed | 2021 |
| LNER Thompson Brake Corridor Composite | Eastern | Ellis Clark/Darstaed | 2021 |
| LNER Thompson Restaurant Buffet | Eastern | Ellis Clark/Darstaed | 2021 |
| BR Mk 1 BSK | All | Dapol/Lionheart Trains | 2020 |
| BR Mk 1 SK | All | Dapol/Lionheart Trains | 2020 |
| BR Mk 1 CK | All | Dapol/Lionheart Trains | 2020 |
| BR Mk 1 SO | All | Dapol/Lionheart Trains | 2020 |
| BR Mk 1 CCT | All | Heljan | TBA |
| BR Mk 2 FK | All | Heljan | 2021 |
| BR Mk 2 TSO | All | Heljan | 2021 |
| BR Mk 2 BSO | All | Heljan | 2021 |
| BR Mk 2 BFK | All | Heljan | 2021 |
| BR Conflat wagon and containers | Various | Dapol | 2020 |
| BR Bogie Bolster E | Midland/Eastern | Dapol | 2020 |
| BR Presflo cement hopper | Various | Ellis Clark Trains | 2021 |
| HEA four-wheel hopper | Various | Dapol | TBA |
| VEA four-wheel van | Various | Dapol | TBA |
| ZZA snowplough | Various | Flangeway/Dapol | TBA |
| Total: 27 | | | |

Due next for 'OO9' is Heljan's model of unique Baldwin 2-4-2T *Lyn* from the Lynton and Barnstaple Railway.

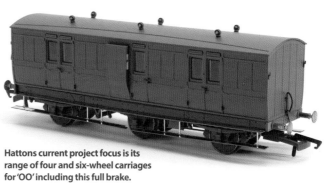

Hattons current project focus is its range of four and six-wheel carriages for 'OO' including this full brake.

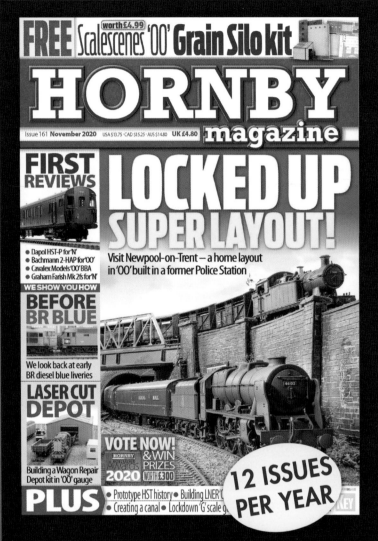

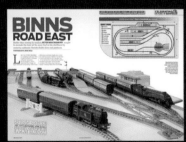

# Acknowledgments

In conceiving and writing this study over a period of seven years or so, too many debts have accumulated as for me to recall them all. Portions of the manuscript often first saw light of day as tentative plots for lectures and points of discussion in my graduate and advanced undergraduate seminars at Duke University. Thus the first debt of gratitude goes to the many brilliant students whose thoughtful questionings have helped the following arguments attain at least some measure of cogency and plausibility. Of these students, I particularly thank Janelle Blankenship, Katey Castellano, Rami Dajani, Charles del Dotto, Kevin Eubanks, Alexander Glage, Jinan Joudeh, Jacques Khalip, Sean Moore, Beau Mount, Magdalena Ostas, and Cara Weber for their perceptive and engaged comments and questions in a number of seminars here at Duke.

I owe a very special debt to Ken Calhoon, Jonathan Skolnik, and Tres Pyle, as well as numerous other faculty and graduate students at the University of Oregon, for their gracious hospitality and thoughtful responses to two presentations of mine on Wordsworth and Heine. I am similarly indebted to faculty and graduate students at the University of Washington and at Carnegie Mellon University for their incisive comments and suggestions in response to my presentations on Kantian aesthetics and Keatsian melancholy; such forums represent our profession at its very best and my book has benefited enormously from these intellectual engagements. Among the many friends and colleagues in the profession whose suggestions have greatly enriched my thinking about this book, I particularly wish to express my lasting gratitude to Ian Balfour, Stephen C. Behrendt, Marshall Brown, Eduardo Cadava, David Clark, Angela Esterhammer, Jerry Hogle, Robert Kaufman, Raimona Modiano, Tilotttama Rajan, Marc Redfield, Karen Weisman, Liliane Weissberg, David Wellbery, and Deborah Elise White.

Finally, among my colleagues whose unwavering professional, intellectual, and personal support and encouragement have meant so much to me throughout my years at Duke, I particularly want to thank Ian Baucom, Sarah

Beckwith, Tom Ferraro, Frank Lentricchia, Rob Mitchell, Michael Valdez Moses, Maureen Quilligan, and Ann Marie Rasmussen. Among all my colleagues, I am especially indebted to David Aers, who not only read and thought through the entire manuscript but has also, throughout my years at Duke, exemplified for me an earnest and capacious outlook on collegial life and meaningful work in today's humanities. I also wish to thank Michael Lonegro for seeing this project through so reliably and efficiently, as well as Peter Dreyer for being so thoughtful and intellectually engaged in preparing the manuscript for print.

By far the most complex and profound debt of gratitude, however, I owe to my wife, Sandra M. Cotton, who, for the past four years, has been a constant and vocal source of inspiration and guidance to me in times of commotion and peace alike. I dedicate this book to her with enduring love.

Portions of this book have previously appeared in the *Modern Language Quarterly 60*, no. 3 (1999), and "Conjuring History: Lyric Cliché, Conservative Fantasy, and Traumatic Awakening in German Romanticism," in *Afterlives of Romanticism*, edited by Ian Baucom, *South Atlantic Quarterly*, Winter 2003, 53–92, and are reprinted here by kind permission of the publishers, Duke University Press. Material adapted from Thomas Pfau, "Paranoia Historicized: Legal Fantasy, Social Change, and Satiric Meta-Commentary in the 1794 Treason Trials," in *Romanticism, Radicalism, and the Press*, edited by Stephen C. Behrendt (1997), 30–64, is used with the kind permission of Wayne State University Press, Detroit, Michigan 48202. Copyright © 1997 by Wayne State University Press. Material adapted from Thomas Pfau, "*Nachtigallenwahnsinn* and *Rabbinismus*: Heine's Literary Provocation to German-Jewish Cultural Identity," in *Romantic Poetry*, edited by Angela Esterhammer (2002), 443–60, is used with the kind permission of John Benjamins Publishing Company, Amsterdam/Philadelphia, www.benjamins.com.

# List of Abbreviations

AGS   Theodor Adorno, *Gesammelte Schriften,* 20 vols. (Darmstadt: Wissenschaftliche Buchgesellschaft, 1998)

CPP   William Blake, *The Complete Poetry and Prose,* ed. David V. Erdman (New York: Anchor Books, 1982)

CrJ   Immanuel Kant, *Critique of Judgment,* trans. J. H. Bernard (New York: Hafner, 1951)

EW   Joseph von Eichendorff, *Werke,* 2 vols. (Düsseldorf: Artemis & Winkler, 1996)

FCH   Sigmund Freud, *Three Case Histories* (New York: Macmillan, 1963)

FSA   Sigmund Freud, *Studienausgabe,* ed. Alexander Mitscherlich (Frankfurt: S. Fischer, 1982)

GCW   William Godwin, *Things as They Are, or, The Adventures of Caleb Wiliams,* ed. Maurice Hindle (Harmondsworth, U.K.: Penguin Books, 1988)

GPJ   William Godwin, *Enquiry Concerning Political Justice* (1798 version), ed. Isaac Kramnick (Harmondsworth, U.K.: Penguin Books, 1985)

HB   *Heinrich Heine: Briefe,* ed. Friedrich Hirth (Mainz: Kupferberg, 1950–51)

HSS   Heinrich Heine, *Sämtliche Schriften,* ed. Klaus Briegleb (Munich: dtv, 1997)

HSW   *The Selected Writings of William Hazlitt,* ed. Duncan Wu, 9 vols. (London: Pickering & Chatto, 1998)

KCP   John Keats, *The Complete Poems,* ed. Miriam Allott (London: Longmans, 1970)

LJK   *Letters of John Keats,* ed. Hyder E. Rollins, 2 vols. (Cambridge, Mass.: Harvard University Press, 1958)

RM   Thomas Paine, *The Rights of Man,* ed. Eric Foner (Harmondsworth, U.K.: Penguin Books, 1984)

SK   Johann Gottlieb Fichte, *The Science of Knowledge,* ed. Peter Heath and John Lachs (New York: Appleton Crofts, 1970)

STT   *A Complete Collection of State Trials and Proceedings for High Treason and Other Crimes and Misdemeanors from the Earliest Period to the Year 1783,* compiled by T. B. Howell (London: T. C. Hansard for Longman, Hurst, Rees, Orme, and Brown [etc.], 1816–28).

WTB   Novalis [Friedrich von Hardenberg], *Werke, Tagebücher, Briefe,* ed. Hans-Joachim Mähl, 3 vols. (Munich: Hanser, 1978)

Romantic Moods